THE
BAD
SPELLER'S
DICTIONARY

BY JOSEPH KREVISKY
AND JORDAN L. LINFIELD

RANDOM HOUSE
NEW YORK

1986 Printing

Library of Congress catalog card number 67-14465.

INTRODUCTION

All of us have trouble, at one time or another, with our spelling. This book is designed for those of you who are bright, educated, and hold responsible positions, but who are—let's face it—bad spellers. If you are a secretary, you know how often your boss makes a mistake in spelling; if you are a student, you know that even your teacher or professor misspells. Doctors, lawyers, Indian chiefs, even presidents are known to misspell. Why?

IT'S OUR ENGLISH LANGUAGE

If you're unsure of your spelling, it is by no means your fault. It's due to the fact that very often there is no rhyme or reason for the spelling of a great many words in the English language.

As an example, take the sound of the letter f. It can be spelled gh, ph, ft, as well as f. The following words illustrate the above variations.

enough   phone   often   fun

None other than George Bernard Shaw created the following spellings, just to point out the inconsistencies in our language:

fish—GHOTI
potato—GHOUGHPTEIGHBTEAU

Stumped? Here's the solution—

FISH

gh as in enough   o as in women   ti as in nation
Sure enough, it's FISH!

POTATO is even more fun—

p as in hiccough
o as in though
t as in ptomaine
a as in neigh
t as in debt
o as in bureau

HOW TO USE
THE BAD SPELLER'S DICTIONARY

Dictionaries, as you know, are wonderful tools for everyone who reads and writes. There is just one catch: you must know how to spell a word correctly in order to find it in an ordinary dictionary.

Not so with *The Bad Speller's Dictionary*. We have arranged thousands of spelling demons according to their common misspellings. No longer do you have to hunt and seek through many pages for a correct spelling. In *The Bad Speller's Dictionary* you simply look up any word as you think it might be spelled—the correct spelling follows. For example:

The **sergeant** and the **colonel** had ptomaine poisoning. If you wanted to check the spelling of these three words you could spend hours looking them up in the standard dictionary under the headings of:

<blockquote>

sar   ker   to

</blockquote>

We have eliminated this problem entirely. NOW YOU DO NOT HAVE TO KNOW THE CORRECT SPELLING OF A WORD IN ORDER TO FIND IT. Simply look up the word as you think it is spelled in the left-hand column of incorrect spellings. If you are misspelling, you will find the word in alphabetical sequence in the left-hand column with the correct spelling in the right-hand column.

If you do not find it in the incorrect spelling list, you are most likely spelling correctly. To make sure, check your spelling in the **QUICK LIST OF CORRECT SPELLINGS** in the back of the book. Here, all the spelling demons are arranged alphabetically by their correct spellings.

Take the word **sergeant**. Suppose you thought it was spelled **sargent**. Look up the word your way—

Incorrect	**Correct**
sargent	**sergeant**

Or suppose you were in doubt as to the spelling of the word **ptomaine**. You're not sure if the word begins with a **p** or a **t**. You lean towards the **t's** however, and following your inclination you will find—

Incorrect	**Correct**
tomaine	**ptomaine**

If you had looked for **ptomaine** under **p's** you would not have found it because you were spelling it correctly. Just double check in the short alphabetical **QUICK LIST OF CORRECT SPELLINGS** at the end of the book.

LOOK-ALIKES OR SOUND-ALIKES

Very often, spelling mistakes are made because we confuse words which look alike or sound alike. For example **to, too,** and **two;** or **it's** and **its.** We have arranged hundreds of such troublesome pairs in the **Look-Alikes or Sound-Alikes** sections of this book, which are found at the end of each letter of the alphabet. A brief definition or key identifying word is given, so that you know immediately which word to use and spell correctly.

SOURCES OF THE WORDS

Some of you may be amazed at the extent and types of spelling errors found in *The Bad Speller's Dictionary.* You might even scoff: "Nobody spells like that!" But those of you who have been exposed to correspondence, stories, advertisements, and articles know just how bad the situation is. The misspellings in this book were compiled from real-life examples in students' tests and essays, office correspondence, ads, articles and stories in print and in manuscript, signs, official notices, and in studies of spelling. The headline writer who wrote about teenagers sniffing "viles" of glue (see our look-alikes and sound-alikes) may be saying more with his misspelling than with correct spelling, but it is still wrong. This is just one of the hundreds upon hundreds of clippings in our files. In fact, we couldn't use many of the words we have collected because of space, and because we felt some were beyond belief. We welcome from the users of *The Bad Speller's Dictionary* examples of misspelling not found in this book.

It is interesting that there is no single pattern of misspelling. This may be one reason why there is a paucity of literature dealing with the causes of spelling errors. We know that phonetic spelling is a key source, but it is far from the only one. Regional speech dialects, transposition of letters, and illogic, all play their role, but a definitive

v

study on the causes of misspelling is yet to be done.

A WORD OF CAUTION

Too often we misspell words without ever realizing it. Therefore, every once in a while, check a spelling even though you think it is correct. You might be surprised.

Keep *The Bad Speller's Dictionary* close at hand. It should be on your desk, at your typewriter, in your briefcase. Refer to it whenever you are in doubt.

Incidentally, try it on your family or friends one night when the TV set is broken.

A

Incorrect	Correct	Incorrect	Correct
abbandon	**abandon**	accownt	**account**
abbolition	**abolition**	accrew	**accrue**
abcess	**abscess**	accrobat	**acrobat**
abdeman	**abdomen**	accross	**across**
abillity	**ability**	accrostic	**acrostic**
abiss	**abyss**	accseed	**accede**
abreviate	**abbreviate**	accumen	**acumen**
abrup	**abrupt**	accur	**occur**
absalutuly	**absolutely**	accurecy	**accuracy**
abscence	**absence**	accurit	**accurate**
abserd	**absurd**	accute	**acute**
absess	**abscess**	acend	**ascend**
absint	**absent**	acer	**acre**
abuze	**abuse**	acertain	**ascertain**
abzurd	**absurd**	acheive	**achieve**
accademic	**academic**	acknowledgement	**acknowledgment**
acceed	**accede**	ackwire	**acquire**
accellarate	**accelerate**	aclimate	**acclimate**
accerasy	**accuracy**	acnowledge	**acknowledge**
accidently	**accidentally**	acommodate	**accommodate**
acclame	**acclaim**	acompany	**accompany**
accnowledge	**acknowledge**	acomplice	**accomplice**
accomodate	**accommodate**	acomplish	**accomplish**
accoustics	**acoustics**	acord	**accord**
		acording	**according**

1

Incorrect	Correct	Incorrect	Correct
acordion	**accordion**	addement	
acost	**accost**		**— adamant**
acount	**account**	addhere	**adhere**
acountent		addick	**addict**
	— accountant	addministeration	
acquantence			**— administration**
	— acquaintance	addmiral	**admiral**
acquasition		addmit	**admit**
	— acquisition	addorible	
acquitle	**acquittal**		**— adorable**
acrabat	**acrobat**	addult	**adult**
acredit	**accredit**	adelesense	
acrege	**acreage**		**— adolescence**
acrew	**accrue**	Adenower	
acros	**across**		**— Adenauer**
acrost	**across**	adequatly	
acrue	**accrue**		**— adequately**
acsesery	**accessory**	adged	**aged**
acshual	**actual**	adict	**addict**
acsident	**accident**	adige	**adage**
acter	**actor**	adishon	**edition**
actualy	**actually**	adition	**addition**
acuire	**acquire**	adjatent	**adjutant**
acumenacal		adjustible	
	— ecumenical		**— adjustable**
acumulate		admendment	
	— accumulate		**— amendment**
acuse	**accuse**	admerable	
acustom	**accustom**		**— admirable**
acuze	**accuse**	administrater	
acwitt	**acquit**		**— administrator**
adaquete		admissable	
	— adequate		**— admissible**

2

Incorrect	Correct	Incorrect	Correct
admitance		aforizm	aphorism
	admittance	afrade	afraid
admition	admission	Africer	Africa
adolesent		afront	affront
	adolescent	afterwerds	
adop	adopt		afterwards
adress	address	agast	aghast
advanse	advance	ageing	aging
advantagous		agencys	agencies
	advantageous	agenst	against
advantige		agensy	agency
	advantage	agern	adjourn
advertisment		agervate	aggravate
	advertisement	aggragate	
advertize	advertise		aggregate
advisery	advisory	aggrarian	agrarian
advizable	advisable	aggree	agree
advizer	adviser	aggresive	
aeriel	aerial		aggressive
afair	affair	aggriculture	
afect	affect		agriculture
affraid	afraid	agground	aground
Affrica	Africa	aginst	against
Afgan	Afghan	agrandize	
afible	affable		aggrandize
afidavit	affidavit	agravate	aggravate
afiliate	affiliate	agreable	agreeable
afirm	affirm	agregate	aggregate
afix	affix	agreing	agreeing
aflict	afflict	agressive	
afluence	affluence		aggressive
aford	afford	ahmond	almond

3

Incorrect	Correct	Incorrect	Correct
aile	aisle	alkohol	alcohol
airea	area	alledge	allege
aireel	aerial	allee	alley
airis	heiress	allegy	allergy
airoplane	aeroplane	allert	alert
		allie	ally
aithe	eighth	allmanac	almanac
ajacent	adjacent		
ajenda	agenda	allmighty	almighty
ajurn	adjourn		
ajustable	adjustable	allmost	almost
		allone	alone
ajutent	adjutant	allotting	alloting
ake	ache	allottment	allotment
aker	acre		
aklaim	acclaim	aloted	allotted
akne	acne	allowence	allowance
akseed	acceed		
aksent	accent	allready	already
akses	axis	allso	also
aksess	access	allthough	although
akward	awkward		
aleby	alibi	alltogether	altogether
aleet	elite		
alege	allege	alluminum	aluminum
alegiance	allegiance		
		allways	always
alergy	allergy	alocate	allocate
aleveate	alleviate	alot	allot
alfabet	alphabet	alow	allow
alian	alien	alowed	allowed
aliance	alliance	alright	all right
aline	align	altenate	alternate

4

Incorrect	Correct	Incorrect	Correct
altrueizm		ammiable	
	— altruism		— amiable
amada —	armada	ammity —	amity
amature —	amateur	amyable —	amiable
ambbasador		analasis —	analysis
	— ambassador	analise —	analyze
ambbiguous		anartic —	antarctic
	— ambiguous	anaversary	
ambulence			— anniversary
	— ambulance	anceint —	ancient
amealiorate		anex	annex
	— ameliorate	angziety —	anxiety
amerous —	amorous	anihilate	
amissable			— annihilate
	— admissible	aniversery	
ammend —	amend		— anniversary
Ammerican		ankel	ankle
	— American	anker	anchor
ammonition		ankshus —	anxious
	— ammunition	annalasis —	analysis
ammonya		annalog —	analog
	— ammonia	annalogy —	analogy
ammount —	amount	annecdote	
amond —	almond		— anecdote
amonia —	ammonia	annew	anew
amoor	amour	annoint —	anoint
amoung —	among	annonymous	
amunition			— anonymous
	— ammunition	anntena —	antenna
amusment		annuel —	annual
	— amusement	annull —	annul
aminable		anonimus	
	— amenable		— anonymous

5

Incorrect	Correct	Incorrect	Correct
anotate — annotate		aparel — apparel	
anouncement — announcement		aparent — apparent	
anoyence — annoyance		apeal — appeal	
anser — answer		apear — appear	
ansester — ancestor		apease — appease	
ansestree — ancestry		apeerence — appearance	
anshent — ancient		apellate — appellate	
antartic — antarctic		apendectomy — appendectomy	
antchovy — anchovy		apendix — appendix	
ante-American — anti-American		apetite — appetite	
antebiotic — antibiotic		aplaud — applaud	
anteek — antique		apliance — appliance	
antisapate — anticipate		aplicant — applicant	
antisedent — antecedent		aply — apply	
anual — annual		apoint — appoint	
anualee — annually		apoligize — apologize	
anuity — annuity		apologeticly — apologetically	
anull — annul		apologys — apologies	
anuther — another		aposle — apostle	
anwser — answer		apparentally — apparently	
anytime — any time		appartment — apartment	
any where — anywhere		appeel — appeal	
aparatus — apparatus			

6

Incorrect	Correct	Incorrect	Correct
appellete		aprin	apron
	— appellate	aproach	
appere	appear		— approach
apperence		apropo	apropos
	— appearance	apropriate	
applys	applies		— appropriate
appointy		aprove	approve
	— appointee	aproximate	
appologize			— approximate
	— apologize	aquaintance	
appology	apology		— acquaintance
appostrophe		aquire	acquire
	— apostrophe	aquisition	
appraisel			— acquisition
	— appraisal	aquittal	acquittal
aprecot	apricot	araign	arraign
appreshiate		arange	arrange
	— appreciate	arbatrate	
appresible			— arbitrate
	— appreciable	arbitery	arbitrary
approove		ardvark	aardvark
	— approve	aready	already
appropo	apropos	arears	arrears
apptitude		arest	arrest
	— aptitude	argueing	arguing
apraise	appraise	arguement	
apreciate			— argument
	— appreciate	arial	aerial
aprehend		ariseing	arising
	— apprehend	arithmatic	
aprentice			— arithmetic
	— apprentice	arive	arrive

7

Incorrect	Correct	Incorrect	Correct
arize	arise	artry	artery
arkaic	archaic	asanine	asinine
Arkansaw		asassin	assassin
	Arkansas	asassinate	
arkitect	architect		assassinate
arkives	archives	asault	assault
armastice		ase	ace
	armistice	asemble	
armfull	armful		assemble
arodynamics		asent	assent
	aerodynamics	asert	assert
arogant	arrogant	asess	assess
Aron	Aaron	aset	asset
aronautics		asfalt	asphalt
	aeronautics	ashin	ashen
arosol	aerosol	ashure	assure
arouseing		asid	acid
	arousing	asign	assign
arow	arrow	asist	assist
arowse	arouse	asistent	assistant
arragent	arrogant	asma	asthma
arrangment		asociate	associate
	arrangement	asort	assort
arrise	arise	aspirent	aspirant
arrivel	arrival	asprin	aspirin
arround	around	assale	assail
arrouse	arouse	assesed	assessed
artaficial	artificial	assimilateable	
artic	arctic		assimilable
artical	article	assine	assign
artilery	artillery	assinine	asinine
artisticly		assistence	
	artistically		assistance

8

Incorrect	Correct	Incorrect	Correct
assylum — asylum	atlete —— athlete
ast ———— asked	atmisfere
astablish	— atmosphere
— establish	atorney — attorney
asternot	atract ——— attract
— astronaut	atrosity —— atrocity
asume —— assume	attatude — attitude
asure —— assure	attemp —— attempt
asurence	aturney — attorney
— assurance	audable — audible
atach ——— attach	audiance
atack ——— attack	— audience
atact ——— attacked	Augest —— August
atain ——— attain	aukward
atempt —— attempt	— awkward
atemt — attempt	aunatomy
atend —— attend	— anatomy
atendence	aunuled — annulled
— attendance	autamatic
atendent	— automatic
— attendant	autamoblie
atenshun	— automobile
— attention	auther —— author
atest ——— attest	automashun
athalete — athlete	— automation
athaletic	auxilary — auxiliary
— athletic	avalable — available
athority — authority	avantage
athyist —— atheist	— advantage
atic ———— attic	aveater —— aviator
atire ——— attire	aved ———— avid
atitude — attitude	avilanch
	— avalanche

Incorrect	Correct	Incorrect	Correct
avocate	advocate	awt	ought
avoidible		awthentick	
	avoidable		authentic
avrage	average	awthorety	
aw	awe		authority
awdiance		awtimaticly	
	audience		automatically
awditoriem		awtum	autumn
	auditorium	axes	axis
awefel	awful	axident	accident
awf	off	aypron	apron
awkwid	awkward	aytheist	atheist
aw revoir		Azher	Asia
	au revoir	azma	asthma

Look-Alikes or Sound-Alikes

Abel (name) · **able** (strong)

abjure (renounce) · **adjure** (entreat)

accede (agree) · **exceed** (go beyond)

accept (receive) · **except** (omit)

accent (speech) · **ascent** (rise) · **assent** (agree)

access (admittance) · **excess** (extra)

acentric (not centered) · **eccentric** (strange)

acerb (bitter) · **a Serb** (a Yugoslav)

acts (to perform on stage, a thing done) · **axe** (tool)

Adam (name) · **atom** (small particle)

adapt (make fit) · **adept** (expert) · **adopt** (take in)

addable (can be added) · **edible** (can be eaten)

addition (add) · **edition** (issue)

adds (increases) · **ads** (advertisements) · **adz** (tool)

adieu (farewell) · **ado** (commotion)

adjoin (next to) · **adjourn** (put off)

adjure (entreat) · **abjure** (renounce)

ado (commotion) · **adieu** (farewell)

ads (advertisements) · **adz** (a cutting tool) · **adds** (increases)

adverse (against) · **averse** (unwilling)

advice (suggestion) · **advise** (to suggest)

10

adz (a cutting tool) · ads (advertisements) · adds (increases)

aerie (eagle's nest) · eerie (ghostly) · eery (eerie) · Erie (the lake)

affect (act or influence) · effect (result of action or to bring about)

affective (emotional) · effective (impressive, operative)

aid (help) · aide (assistant)

aigrette (ornamental plume) · · egret (heron)

ail (to be ill) · ale (drink)

air (gas) · e'er (ever) · heir (inheritor)

aisle (passage) · I'll (I will) · isle (island)

allay (calm) · alley (lane) · ally (friend) · alloy (composed of two metals)

all ready (adj., completely prepared) · already (adv., before now)

allowed (permitted) · aloud (spoken)

allude (refer to) · elude (escape)

allusion (reference to) · illusion (false impression)

allusive (referring to) · elusive (evasive) · illusive (deceptive)

alms (charity) · arms (body)

already (adv., before now) · all ready (adj., completely prepared)

altar (church) · alter (change)

alternate (first one, then the other) · alternative (one without the other)

alternative (one without the other) · alternate (first one, then the other)

altitude (height) · attitude (point of view)

amiable (describing a personality) · amicable (describing a relationship)

amicable (describing a relationship) · amiable (describing a personality)

amoral (without a sense of moral responsibility) · immoral (evil)

angel (heavenly) · angle (mathematics)

ant (insect) · aunt (relative)

ante (before) · anti (against) · aunty (relative)

anyone ([pronoun] is anyone there?) · any one ([adj.] I'd like any one of those girls.)

apatite (mineral) · appetite (craving)

appetite (craving) · apatite (mineral)

apposite (appropriate) · opposite (contrary)

appraise (to judge) · apprise (inform) · a prize (a reward)

arc (curved line) · ark (vessel) · arch (building)

area (portion of land) · aria (opera selection)

aria (opera selection) · area (portion of land)

arms (body) · alms (charity)

arraign (accuse) · arrange (settle)

a Serb (a Yugoslav) · acerb (bitter)

ascent (rise) · assent (agree) · accent (speech)

assay (evaluate) · essay (composition)

assent (agree) · ascent (rise) · accent (speech)

assistance (help) · assistants (people who help)

11

assurance (certainty) ·
insurance (protection)

ate (did eat) · eight (the
number)

attach (bind) · attaché (aide) ·
attack (assault)

attendance (act of attending) ·
attendants (people who attend)

attitude (point of view) ·
altitude (height)

aught (zero) · ought (should)

aunt (relative) · ant (insect)

aural (hearing) · oral (verbal)

autarchy (autocratic rule) ·
autarky (national economic
self-sufficiency)

automation (electronics) ·
automaton (robot)

averse (unwilling) · adverse
(against)

awe (fear) · oar (boat) · o'er
(over) · or (alternative) ·
ore (mineral)

awhile ([adverb] use without
"for") · a while ([noun] he
stayed for a while)

axes (tools) · axis (line)

aye (yes) · eye (see) · I (me

12

B

Incorrect	Correct	Incorrect	Correct
bachler	bachelor	bannana	banana
backinal	bacchanal	baptise	baptize
backround	background	baracks	barracks
backwerd	backward	barage	barrage
bagage	baggage	barate	berate
bagan	began	barbacue	barbecue
bage	badge	barell	barrel
bagin	begin	bargin	bargain
baid	bade	barikade	barricade
baige	beige	barly	barley
baist	baste	basicly	basically
bakon	bacon	basik	basic
balay	ballet	basiz	basis
balence	balance	bastid	bastard
balistics	ballistics	batallian	battalion
balital	belittle	batchler	bachelor
ballid	ballad	batray	betray
ballit	ballot	battry	battery
bamy	balmy	baught	bought
bandige	bandage	bawk	balk
baner	banner	baygel	bagel
banista	banister	beatle	beetle
banjoes	banjos	beautyful	beautiful
bankrup	bankrupt	becomeing	becoming
bankrupcy	bankruptcy	becon	beacon
		becum	become

13

Incorrect	Correct	Incorrect	Correct
becuz	because	bequethe	bequeath
bedder	better	beray	beret
beever	beaver	berbin	bourbon
beeware	beware	berden	burden
befor	before	bergler	burglar
beger	beggar	berglery	burglary
beginer	beginner	berial	burial
begining		beriel	burial
	beginning	berlap	burlap
behavier		berlesk	burlesque
	behavior	Berma	Burma
beir	bier	bernt	burnt
beleaf	belief	berrser	bursar
beleive	believe	berser	bursar
beligerant		berst	burst
	belligerent	beseige	besiege
belitel	belittle	beserk	berserk
bely	belie	bestyal	bestial
benafit	benefit	beuty	beauty
bended	bent	Bibel	Bible
benefishal		biege	beige
	beneficial	bigest	biggest
benefishery		biggamy	bigamy
	beneficiary	biggot	bigot
beneith	beneath	bild	build
benevelent		bilet	billet
	benevolent	biliard	billiard
benifited		bilion	billion
	benefited	billyus	bilious
benine	benign	bilt	built
beogrephy		binery	binary
	biography	binnoculars	
beond	beyond		binoculars

14

Incorrect	Correct	Incorrect	Correct
birden	burden	blugen	bludgeon
birdy	birdie	blujen	bludgeon
bisek	biseet	boch	botch
biseps	biceps	boddy	body
biskit	biscuit	boid	bird
bisy	busy	boistrous	
biter	bitter		boisterous
bivwak	bivouac	bolstir	bolster
bizness	business	bom	bomb
blair	blare	bomy	balmy
blakgard		bondfire	bonfire
	blackguard	bonet	bonnet
blamful	blameful	boney	bony
blamless		bonion	bunion
	blameless	bonis	bonus
blankit	blanket	bon swar	
blasay	blasé		bon soir
blasfemy		boodwar	boudoir
	blasphemy	booey	buoy
bleech	bleach	bookay	bouquet
bleek	bleak	bookeeping	
blest	blessed		bookkeeping
bleve	believe	boorzhwa	
blite	blight		bourgeois
blith	blithe	boosom	bosom
blits	blitz	bord	board
blizard	blizzard	borow	borrow
blockaid		bost	boast
	blockade	bosun	boatswain
blok	block	bosy	bossy
bloter	blotter	botom	bottom
blowse	blouse	bottel	bottle
bluf	bluff	boundry	boundary

15

Incorrect	Correct	Incorrect	Correct
bouyant —	buoyant	bronkiel —	
boycot —	boycott		— bronchial
bracke —	brake	browz —	browse
brade —	braid	bruk —	brook
bragart —	braggart	bruz —	bruise
brane —	brain	buckel —	buckle
bran-new —		bucksome —	buxom
	— brand-new	Buda —	Buddha
braselet —	bracelet	buety —	beauty
bravry —	bravery	bufalo —	buffalo
brazere —	brassiere	bufer —	buffer
breakible —		buffay —	buffet
	— breakable	bufoon —	buffoon
bredth —	breadth	buge —	budge
breif —	brief	bugel —	bugle
brekfast —		bujet —	budget
	— breakfast	buket —	bucket
brest —	breast	buksom —	buxom
brethern —		buldozer —	
	— brethren		— bulldozer
brez —	breeze	bulit —	bullet
brigader —		bulitin —	bulletin
	— brigadier	bullivard —	
brige —	bridge		— boulevard
briliant —	brilliant	bullyon —	bouillon
Britanica —		bumbelbee —	
	— Britannica		— bumblebee
brite —	bright	bunglow —	
Britin —	Britain		— bungalow
brocalli —	broccoli	burbin —	bourbon
brokin —	broken	burch —	birch
brokrage —		burglery —	burglary
	— brokerage	buriel —	burial

16

Incorrect	Correct	Incorrect	Correct
buro	**bureau**	busyly	**busily**
busibody		butician	
	busybody		**beautician**
busness	**business**	butiful	**beautiful**
busom	**bosom**	butten	**button**
bussel	**bustle**	bycycle	**bicycle**

Look-Alikes or Sound-Alikes

babble (chatter) · **bauble** (trifle) · **bubble** (as in soap bubbles)

bad (no good) · **bade** (asked)

bail (security) · **bale** (bundle)

bait (a lure) · **bate** (lessen)

bald (no hair) · **balled** (put in ball) · **bawled** (cried)

ballad (song, poem) · **ballet** (dance) · **ballot** (vote)

balm (ointment) · **bomb** (explosive)

baloney (bunk) · **bologna** (sausage)

band (ring; orchestra) · **banned** (barred)

banns (marriage) · **bands** (groups) · **bans** (prohibits)

bard (poet) · **barred** (stopped)

bare (naked) · **bear** (carry, animal)

baring (exposing) · **bearing** (carriage; support)

baron (noble) · **barren** (empty)

base (foundation) · **bass** (deep tone)

bases (foundations; stations) · **basis** (the groundwork)

bate (lessen) · **bait** (lure)

bath (the noun) · **bathe** (the verb)

bathos (anticlimax) · **pathos** (tender)

bauble (trifle) · **babble** (chatter) · **bubble** (as in soap bubble)

baud (unit of telegraph signal speed) · **bawd** (a procuress)

bawd (a procuress) · **baud** (unit of telegraph signal speed)

bawled (cried) · **bald** (no hair) · **balled** (put in a ball)

bazaar (a fair) · **bizarre** (weird)

be (exist) · **bee** (insect)

beach (shore) · **beech** (tree)

bean (vegetable) · **been** (past of be) · **bin** (box)

bear (carry or animal) · **bare** (naked)

bearing (carriage or support) · **baring** (exposing)

beat (strike) · **beet** (vegetable)

beatify (make happy; religious act) · **beautify** (make beautiful)

beau (dandy; lover) · **bow** (arrow)

bee (insect) · **be** (exist)

beech (tree) · **beach** (shore)

been (past of be) · **bean** (vegetable) · **bin** (box)

17

beer (drink) · bier (coffin)

bell (rings) · belle (beauty)

bellow (pumps air) · below (under)

below (under) · bellow (pumps air)

berry (fruit) · bury (to cover)

berth (place to sleep) · birth (born)

beseech (beg) · besiege (surround, in war)

beside (at the side of) · besides (in addition to)

besiege (surround, in war) · beseech (beg)

better (more than good) · bettor (one who bets)

biannual (twice a year) · biennial (every two years)

bib (shield tied under chin) · bibb (nautical term, part of mast)

bid (request) · bide (wait)

bide (wait) · bid (request)

biennial (every two years) · biannual (twice a year)

billed (sent a bill) · build (construct)

bin (box) · been (part of be) · bean (vegetable)

birth (born) · berth (place to sleep)

bizarre (weird) · bazaar (a fair)

blanch (whiten) · Blanche (name)

Blanche (name) · blanch (whiten)

blew (wind; breath) · blue (color)

bloc (political group) · block (solid piece, prevent)

boar (swine) · bore (drill, dull)

board (lumber or climb on) · bored (weary)

boarder (roomer) · border (edge)

bold (daring) · bowled (did bowl)

bolder (braver) · boulder (big rock)

bole (clay; tree trunk) · boll (weevil) · bowl (dish; game)

bologna (food) · baloney (bunk) · Bologna (Italian city)

bomb (explosive) · balm (ointment)

born (given birth) · borne (carried)

borne (carried) · born (given birth)

borough (town) · burro (donkey) · burrow (hole, dig)

bough (tree) · bow (bend, yield)

bouillon (soup) · bullion (gold, silver)

boulder (big rock) · bolder (braver)

bow (arrow) · beau (lover)

bowl (dish; game) · bole (clay; tree trunk) · boll (weevil)

bowled (did bowl) · bold (daring)

boy (lad) · buoy (a float)

braes (hillsides) · brays (utters harsh sounds) · braze (to solder)

braid (trim) · brayed (bellowed)

brake (stop) · break (destroy)

brays (utters harsh sounds) · braze (to solder) · braes (hillsides)

braze (to solder) · braes (hillsides) · brays (utters harsh sounds)

breach (break; violation) · breech (bottom)

bread (food) · bred (raised)

18

breadth (expanse) · **breath** (air inhaled) · **breathe** (to inhale and exhale)

breath (air inhaled) · **breathe** (to inhale and exhale) · **breadth** (expanse)

breathe (to inhale and exhale) · **breath** (air inhaled) · **breadth** (expanse)

brewed (liquor) · **brood** (offspring; worry)

brews (makes liquor) · **bruise** (wound)

briar (pipe wood) · **brier** (thorny bush)

bridal (wedding) · **bridle** (restrain; horse)

brier (thorny bush) · **briar** (pipe wood)

broach (tool; discuss) · **brooch** (a clasp)

brows (foreheads) · **browse** (read here and there)

bruit (rumor) · **brute** (savage)

bubble (as in soap bubble) · **bauble** (trifle) · **babble** (chatter)

build (construct) · **billed** (sent a bill)

bullion (gold, silver) · **bouillon** (soup)

buoy (support) · **boy** (lad)

burley (a thin-bodied tobacco) · **burly** (large, muscular)

burly (large, muscular) · **burley** (a thin-bodied tobacco)

burro (donkey) · **burrow** (hole, dig) · **borough** (town)

bury (put in ground) · **berry** (fruit)

but (however) · **butt** (end, object)

buy (purchase) · **by** (near) · **bye** (sport)

19

C

Incorrect	Correct	Incorrect	Correct
cabage	**cabbage**	camelia	**camellia**
cabanet	**cabinet**	cameradery	
cabel	**cable**		**— camaraderie**
cach	**catch**	camfer	**camphor**
cafeine	**caffeine**	canvis	**canvas**
caffé	**café**	canyen	**canyon**
caffs	**calves**	caos	**chaos**
calaco	**calico**	capashus	
Calafornia			**— capacious**
	— California	capible	**capable**
caleber	**caliber**	capilary	**capillary**
calender	**calendar**	capitchulate	
calidiscope			**— capitulate**
	— kaleidoscope	capitil	**capital**
calijun	**collision**	cappacity	
calipso	**calypso**		**— capacity**
caliry	**calory**	caprese	**caprice**
calizhun	**collision**	capsel	**capsule**
callamity		capshun	**caption**
	— calamity	captan	**captain**
callisthenics		captin	**captain**
	— calisthenics	caracter	
calocwiel			**— character**
	— colloquial	carbahidrate	
calry	**calorie**		**— carbohydrate**
calsium	**calcium**	carberater	
camafloge			**— carburetor**
	— camouflage	cardiak	**cardiac**
camara	**camera**	cardnil	**cardinal**
camasole	**camisole**	carear	**career**

Incorrect	Correct	Incorrect	Correct
carefull	careful	cashoe	cashew
careing	caring	caskit	casket
caricatour		casmint	casement
	caricature	casock	cassock
caried	carried	cassaroll	
carit	carat		casserole
carm	calm	cassel	castle
carmel	caramel	castagate	
carnivul	carnival		castigate
carnul	carnal	castinet	castanet
caroner	coroner	casulty	casualty
carot	carrot	cataclism	
carowse	carouse		cataclysm
carowz	carouse	catagory	
carress	caress		category
Carribean		catapiller	
	Caribbean		caterpillar
carrige	carriage	catar	catarrh
carring	carrying	catastrofy	
cartalige	cartilage		catastrophe
cart blansh		catelogue	catalog
	carte blanche	cateract	cataract
cartell	cartel	Cathlic	Catholic
cartin	carton	caticomb	
cartridge			catacomb
	cartridge	catilyon	cotillion
cartune	cartoon	catipult	catapult
casarole		catkus	cactus
	casserole	cauff	cough
cascaid	cascade	cavelcaid	
casel	castle		cavalcade
casheer	cashier	caveleir	cavalier
cashmear	cashmere		

Incorrect	Correct	Incorrect	Correct
cavernus	———	certin ——	certain
	— cavernous	chagrinned	———
cawcus ——	caucus		— chagrined
cawk ———	caulk	chaif ———	chafe
cawleflower	———	chaist ———	chaste
	— cauliflower	chalenge	———
cawshun —	caution		— challenge
cawz ———	cause	champeen	———
cazm ———	chasm		— champion
ceder ———	cedar	champoo	———
ceese ———	cease		— shampoo
celabacy —	celibacy	chane ———	chain
celebrait —	celebrate	chanel —	channel
celophane	———	changable	———
	— cellophane		— changeable
celuloid —	celluloid	chaplin —	chaplain
cematary	———	charaty —	charity
	— cemetery	chare ———	chair
cemicle —	chemical	chariet —	chariot
cenchury —	century	chater —	chatter
cencus ——	census	chauffuer	———
centenial	———		— chauffeur
	— centennial	chawk ——	chalk
centor ——	centaur	cheder —	cheddar
centrel ——	central	cheep ——	cheap
centrifigle	———	cheet ———	cheat
	— centrifugal	cheez ——	cheese
cereberal	———	cheif ———	chief
	— cerebral	Chekaslavakia	———
cerfue ——	curfew		— Czechoslovakia
cerimony	———	chelo ———	cello
	— ceremony	chemest —	chemist
		cherib ——	cherub

Incorrect	Correct	Incorrect	Correct
chesnut —	**chestnut**	ciment —	**cement**
Cheverlay		cinamon	
	— **Chevrolet**		— **cinnamon**
chieftin —	**chieftain**	Cinncinatti	
childern —	**children**		— **Cincinnati**
chimny —	**chimney**	circal	**circle**
chinchila		circomstance	
	— **chinchilla**		— **circumstance**
chints —	**chintz**	circuler —	**circular**
chipendale		circumfrence	
	— **Chippendale**		— **circumference**
chivelrus		circumsize	
	— **chivalrous**		— **circumcise**
chizel —	**chisel**	cirkit —	**circuit**
choclit —	**chocolate**	cist —	**cyst**
choffer —	**chauffeur**	citazen —	**citizen**
chossen —	**chosen**	citris —	**citrus**
chow —	**ciao**	cival —	**civil**
chow main		civlisation	
	— **chow mein**		— **civilization**
choyce —	**choice**	clamer —	**clamor**
chrisanthemun		clanish —	**clannish**
— **chrysanthemum**		clarvoiance	
chrisen —	**christen**		— **clairvoyance**
Christyan		clasify —	**classify**
	— **Christian**	clauz —	**clause**
chuby —	**chubby**	clearinse	
chumy —	**chummy**		— **clearance**
cicle —	**cycle**	cleek —	**clique**
ciclone —	**cyclone**	clense —	**cleanse**
cieling —	**ceiling**	cleptamania	
cigret —	**cigarette**		— **kleptomania**
cilynder —	**cylinder**	cleracle —	**clerical**

Incorrect	Correct	Incorrect	Correct
clevige	cleavage	coldslaw	coleslaw
clientell	clientele	colect	collect
clif	cliff	colecter	collector
cliper	clipper	coleegue	
clok	clock		colleague
cloke.	cloak	colege	college
cloraform		colegiate	
	chloroform		collegiate
closh	cloche	coler	color
closit	closet	colera	cholera
cloun	clown	colerachura	
cloyster	cloister		coloratura
cloz	clothes	Coleseum	
clozure	closure		Colosseum
clumzy	clumsy	collapsable	
coam	comb		collapsible
coch	coach	colleck	collect
cocksin	coxswain	colledge	college
coersion	coercion	collegit	collegiate
cofee	coffee	coller	collar
coff	cough	collosal	colossal
cofin	coffin	colloseum	
cohearint			coliseum
	coherent	colonaid	
coinsidence			colonnade
	coincidence	colone	cologne
cojitait	cogitate	colum	column
colaborate		colyumist	
	collaborate		columnist
colapse	collapse	coma	comma
colar	collar	comemorate	
colateral			commemorate
	collateral		

24

Incorrect	Correct	Incorrect	Correct
comendable —		companyon —	
	— **commendable**		— **companion**
comercial —		comparitive —	
	— **commercial**		— **comparative**
comftable —		compatable —	
	— **comfortable**		— **compatible**
comission —		compatense —	
	— **commission**		— **competence**
comit — **commit**		compeet — **compete**	
comited —		compeled —	
	— **committed**		— **compelled**
comittee —		compell — **compel**	
	— **committee**	compermize —	
commedian —			— **compromise**
	— **comedian**	competant —	
commedy — **comedy**			— **competent**
commen —		compinsashun —	
	— **common**		— **compensation**
commendible —		compis — **compass**	
	— **commendable**	compitition —	
commenshurite —			— **competition**
	— **commensurate**	complacate —	
commet — **comet**			— **complicate**
commic — **comic**		complementry —	
comming — **coming**			— **complementary**
comminism —		complexshun —	
	— **communism**		— **complexion**
commision —		complience —	
	— **commission**		— **compliance**
commitee —		composishun —	
	— **committee**		— **composition**
comodity —		compoze —	
	— **commodity**		— **compose**

Incorrect	Correct	Incorrect	Correct
compresed		concreet — **concrete**	
	compressed	concurense	
comprible			**concurrence**
	comparable	concushin	
compulsery			**concussion**
	compulsory	condem — **condemn**	
comred — **comrade**		condesend	
comtroller			**condescend**
	comptroller	condinsashun	
comunicate			**condensation**
	communicate	condishun	
comunity			**condition**
	community	conduck — **conduct**	
comute — **commute**		conect — **connect**	
conasseur		conection	
	connoisseur		**connection**
conceed — **concede**		confadense	
concensus			**confidence**
	consensus	confederit	
concequénce			**confederate**
	consequence	confekshinery	
concer —— **concur**			**confectionery**
conchribeaut		confered— **conferred**	
	contribute	conferm — **confirm**	
concientious		confes —— **confess**	
	conscientious	confinment	
concieve			**confinement**
	conceive	confligrashun	
conclaive			**conflagration**
	conclave	confortable	
concock — **concoct**			**comfortable**
concorse		confrence	
	concourse		**conference**

26

Incorrect	Correct	Incorrect	Correct
Confushus	———	consert ——	concert
	— **Confucius**	conservitory	———
congagate	———		— **conservatory**
	— **conjugate**	consession	———
congell —	congeal		— **concession**
congenyal	———	conshunse	———
	— **congenial**		— **conscience**
congradulate	———	conshuss	———
	— **congratulate**		— **conscious**
congrigashun	———	considrable	———
	— **congregation**		— **considerable**
congrous	———	consinement	———
	— **congruous**		— **consignment**
conjer ——	conjure	consil ———	consul
conjeture	———	consiliate	———
	— **conjecture**		— **conciliate**
conker ——	conquer	consise ——	concise
Connecticut	———	consistant	———
	— **Connecticut**		— **consistent**
connisseur	———	consittar —	consider
	— **connoisseur**	consoladate	———
conotashun	———		— **consolidate**
	— **connotation**	consomate	———
conote ——	connote		— **consummate**
conseal —	conceal	consoul —	console
conseat —	conceit	constible—	constable
conseed —	concede	constilashun	———
conseive —	conceive		— **constellation**
consentrait	———	constint —	constant
	— **concentrate**	consumtion	———
consentrick	———		— **consumption**
	— **concentric**	consynment	———
consept —	concept		— **consignment**

Incorrect	Correct	Incorrect	Correct
contajus		controled	
	contagious		**controlled**
contane	**contain**	controll	**control**
contanent		contry	**country**
	continent	conubeal	
contempry			**connubial**
	contemporary	conviless	
contemt			**convalesce**
	contempt	convilute	
contemtable			**convolute**
	contemptible	convinient	
conterary	**contrary**		**convenient**
contimplate		convirge	
	contemplate		**converge**
continense		convirse	**converse**
	countenance	convirtable	
continnualy			**convertible**
	continually	convolse	**convulse**
continous		conyak	**cognac**
	continuous	coo di gra	
contore	**contour**		**coup de grace**
contractural		cookoo	**cuckoo**
	contractual	cookry	**cookery**
contrarywise		cooly	**coolly**
	contrariwise	coopay	**coupé**
contratan		coopon	**coupon**
	contretemps	cooprate	
contravershil			**cooperate**
	controversial	coper	**copper**
contraversy		copeus	**copious**
	controversy	Copinhagin	
contribeaut			**Copenhagen**
	contribute	cople	**couple**

Incorrect	Correct	Incorrect	Correct
coprate	**cooperate**	corraled	**corralled**
copyriter		corronary	
	copywriter		**coronary**
copywright		corsarge	**corsage**
	copyright	corse	**course**
cor	**corps**	corsit	**corset**
coral	**corral**	cort	**court**
corcage	**corkage**	cortison	
corderoy			**courtesan**
	corduroy	cortmarshal	
cordige	**cordage**		**courtmartial**
cordnation		corz	**corps**
	coordination	cosher	**kosher**
corect	**correct**	costic	**caustic**
corelate	**correlate**	cosy	**cozy**
coreografy		cotage	**cottage**
	choreography	cotin	**cotton**
corespond		counsler	
	correspond		**counselor**
coridor	**corridor**	counterfit	
corigated			**counterfeit**
	corrugated	countes	**countess**
coril	**coral**	courticy	**courtesy**
corn-beef		covrage	**coverage**
	corned beef	cowerd	**coward**
cornise	**cornice**	Cozak	**Cossack**
cornor	**corner**	cozmapolitan	
coroborate			**cosmopolitan**
	corroborate	cozmic	**cosmic**
corperal	**corporal**	cozzin	**cousin**
corpisle	**corpuscle**	craby	**crabby**
corpration		cradenchle	
	corporation		**credential**

29

Incorrect	Correct	Incorrect	Correct
crain	crane	crokay	croquet
craion	crayon	crokete	croquette
crak	crack	cromatizm	
crakel	crackle		chromatism
cramberry		crome	chrome
	cranberry	cronic	chronic
crape	crepe	croocial	crucial
crashendo		crood	crude
	crescendo	crool	cruel
craul	crawl	croopya	croupier
craydal	cradle	croud	crowd
creashun	creation	cround	crowned
credable	credible	crowshay	crochet
credlus	credulous	crsanthemun	
creedence			chrysanthemum
	credence	cruch	crutch
creem	cream	crue	crew
creese	crease	cruely	cruelly
creture	creature	crulty	cruelty
crie	cry	crum	crumb
criket	cricket	crushal	crucial
crimnal	criminal	cruzer	cruiser
crimsin	crimson	cryed	cried
criple	cripple	cubbard	
Crismas	Christmas		cupboard
Cristian	Christian	Cuber	Cuba
cristilize		culcher	culture
	crystallize	culer	color
critacal	critical	cullinary	culinary
criteek	critique	cultavate	
critisise	criticize		cultivate
crokadile		cumand	
	crocodile		command

Incorrect	Correct	Incorrect	Correct
cumense		curley —— **curly**	
	commence	curnel —— **kernel**	
cumfortable		currancy	
	comfortable		**currency**
cuming —— **coming**		curst —— **cursed**	
cuning —— **cunning**		curteous	
cuntry —— **country**			**courteous**
cupon —— **coupon**		custid —— **custard**	
curancy — **currency**		custidy —— **custody**	
curchef — **kerchief**		custimor	
curent —— **current**			**customer**
curiculum		cuver —— **cover**	
	curriculum	cuvinant	
curige —— **courage**			**covenant**
curios —— **curious**		cwafeur —— **coiffure**	
curiousity		cyder —— **cider**	
	curiosity	cypher —— **cipher**	

Look-Alikes or Sound-Alikes

cabal (a secret group) · **cable** (wire)

cable (wire) · **cabal** (a secret group)

cacao (tree of cocoa) · **cocoa** (chocolate)

cache (hiding place) · **cash** (money)

caddie (golf attendant) · **caddy** (tea box)

calendar (time) · **calender** (machine to press)

callous (unfeeling) · **callus** (hard skin)

calm (quiet) · **cam** (machinery part)

Calvary (crucifixion) · **cavalry** (horse troops)

cam (machinery part) · **calm** (quiet)

canon (law) · **cannon** (gun)

cant (dialect) · **can't** (cannot)

canvas (cloth) · **canvass** (to solicit)

capital (main, city) · **Capitol** (the building)

carat (diamond) · **caret** (proofreader's mark) · **carrot** (vegetable)

carousal (orgy) · **carousel** (merry-go-round)

carousel (merry-go-round) · carousal (orgy)

cash (money) · cache (hiding place)

cask (box) · casque (helmet)

casque (helmet) · cask (box)

caster (thrower; turner) · castor (secretion used in medicines)

casual (easy going) · causal (the cause of)

cataclasm (breakage, disruption) · cataclysm (great flood)

cataclysm (great flood) · cataclasm (breakage, disruption)

caught (did catch) · court (law, woo)

cause (to bring about) · caws (the sounds made by crows)

caws (the sounds made by crows) · cause (to bring about)

cease (stop) · seize (grab) · seas (bodies of water) · sees (observes)

cede (give up) · seed (flower)

ceiling (top) · sealing (closing)

cell (prison, unit in biology) · sell (opposite of buy)

cellar (basement) · seller (one who sells)

cemetery (graveyard) · symmetry (even)

censer (for incense) · censor (moral overseer) · censure (condemn)

census (population count) · senses (sight, touch)

cents (money) · scents (smells) · sense (brains)

cereal (food) · serial (in a row)

cession (yielding) · session (meeting)

champagne (wine) · champaign (plain)

champaign (plain) · champagne (wine)

charted (put on a chart) · chartered (rented)

chased (ran after) · chaste (pure)

cheap (priced low) · cheep (sound of young birds)

check (money) · Czech (nationality)

cheep (sound of young bird) · cheap (priced low)

chert (a rock) · shirt (garment)

chews (eats) · choose (select)

chic (stylish) · sheik (Arab chief)

chili (food) · chilly (cold) · Chile (country)

choler (rage) · collar (neckwear) · color (hue)

choral (singing) · coral (sea life) · corral (animal pen)

chord (music) · cord (rope)

christen (baptize) · Christian (a believer in Christ)

Christian (a believer in Christ · christen (baptize)

chute (drop) · shoot (fire)

Cilician (from Cilicia, a province in Asia Minor) · Sicilian (from Sicily, an island off and part of Italy)

cite (point out) · sight (see) · site (place)

clause (contract) · claws (sharp nails)

clench (close teeth) · clinch (to embrace; to conclude a deal)

click (noise) · clique (small group)

climactic (refers to climax) · climatic (refers to climate)

climb (ascent) · clime (climate)

clinch (to embrace; to conclude a deal) · clench (close teeth)

close (shut) · clothes (apparel) · cloths (small fabric)

coal (fire) · kohl (eye shadow) · koel (a cuckoo)

coarse (rough) · course (class; passage)

cockscomb (a garden plant) · coxcomb (fop) · cock's comb (comb of a cock)

cocoa (chocolate) · cacao (tree of cocoa)

cola (a drink) · kola (a nut or tree)

collage (a type of painting) · college (a group, as in education)

collision (crash) · collusion (fraud)

Colombia (a country in South America) · Columbia (the college)

colonel (officer) · kernel (seed)

color (hue) · collar (neckwear) · choler (rage)

Columbia (the college) · Colombia (a country in South America)

comity (welfare) · committee (a group working for a definite purpose)

command (order) · commend (praise)

commendation (praise) · condemnation (denunciation)

committee (a group working for a definite purpose) · comity (welfare)

complacence (self-satisfaction) · complaisance (fulfillment of wishes of others)

complacent (pleased with oneself) · complaisant (desirous of pleasing)

complaisance (fulfillment of wishes of others) · complacence (self-satisfaction)

complaisant (desirous of pleasing) · complacent (pleased with oneself)

complement (balance) · compliment (praise)

comprehensible (understandable) · comprehensive (including much)

comprehensive (including much) · comprehensible (understandable)

condemn (to find guilty) · contemn (to despise)

confidant (a person confided in) · confident (certain)

confident (certain) · confidant (a person confided in)

confirmer (one who ratifies) · conformer (one who complies with established customs)

conformer (one who complies with established customs) · confirmer (one who ratifies)

conscientious (painstaking) · conscious (aware)

conscious (aware) · conscientious (painstaking)

consul (diplomat) · counsel (advice) · council (an assembly)

contemn (to despise) · condemn (to find guilty)

continual (repeated again and again) · continuous (without a break)

continuous (without a break) · continual (repeated again and again)

coolie (laborer) · coolly (in a cool manner)

coral (sea life) · corral (animal pen) · choral (singing)

core (center) · corps (army) · corpse (body)

33

corespondent (paramour in divorce proceedings) · correspondent (one party to exchange of letters) ·

corporal (of the body; a soldier) · corporeal (material; tangible)

corporeal (material; tangible) · corporal (of the body; a soldier)

correspondent (one party to exchange of letters) · corespondent (paramour in divorce proceedings) ·

costume (clothes) · custom (habit)

council (an assembly) · counsel (advice) · consul (diplomat)

councilor (member of council) · counselor (advisor, lawyer)

course (class; passage) · coarse (rough)

court (law) · caught (did catch)

courtesy (manners) · curtsy (bow)

coward (one who lacks courage) · cowered (crouched, shrank)

coxcomb (fop) · cockscomb (a garden plant; comb of a cock)

cousin (a relative) · cozen (to deceive)

cozen (to deceive) · cousin (a relative)

creak (noise) · creek (stream)

crease (fold) · kris (cheese; dagger)

credible (believable) · creditable (praiseworthy)

Cretan (inhabitant of Crete) · cretin (a type of idiot)

crews (sailors) · cruise (voyage)

critic (one who criticizes) · critique (criticism)

crochet (a kind of knitting) · crotchet (a quirk; a hook)

croquet (a game played with mallets, balls) · croquette (a fried cake of minced food)

croquette (a fried cake of minced food) · croquet (a game played with mallets, balls)

cue (hint; billiards) · queue (line)

currant (a berry) · current (refers to a stream of water, or events; contemporary)

current (refers to a stream of water, or events; contemporary) · currant (a berry)

cygnet (a young swan) · signet (a seal)

cymbal (music) · symbol (sign)

Czech (nationality) · check (money)

D

Incorrect	Correct	Incorrect	Correct
dabate	debate	dat	that
dable	dabble	datta	data
dabochery		dauter	daughter
	debauchery	davelop	develop
dacolté	décolleté	daybu	debut
dafodile	daffodil	dayly	daily
dager	dagger	dazel	dazzle
dakiri	daiquiri	debaner	debonair
dakron	dacron	debry	debris
dakshound		debths	depths
	dachshund	decarate	
dalapadate			decorate
	dilapidate	decend	descend
dalia	dahlia	decese	decease
dalinkwent		deciet	deceit
	delinquent	decieve	deceive
daluge	deluge	decleration	
damenshin			declaration
	dimension	decloté	décolleté
damige	damage	decmal	decimal
danderuf		decon	deacon
	dandruff	decreese	
dandylion			decrease
	dandelion	ded	dead
danjros		dedecate	
	dangerous		dedicate
dary	dairy	deductable	
dashund			deductible
	dachshund	deduse	deduce
dassiay	dossier	def	deaf

35

Incorrect	Correct	Incorrect	Correct
defalt	default	Deleware	
defanitely			Delaware
	definitely	delite	delight
defanition		delivry	delivery
	definition	delliberate	
defeet	defeat		deliberate
defence	defense	dellicacy	
defendent			delicacy
	defendant	dellicatessan	
defensable			delicatessen
	defensible	dellicious	
defered	deferred		delicious
defficit	deficit	delt	dealt
defiants	defiance	deluxe	de luxe
defie	defy	demacrat	
definit	definite		democrat
definitly		deminish	
	definitely		diminish
defishent		deminstrate	
	deficient		demonstrate
defiunce	defiance	democrasy	
defnite	definite		democracy
defrence		demogogue	
	deference		demagogue
defyed	defied	demonstratable	
De Gaul			demonstrable
	De Gaulle	demytass	
dehidrate			demi-tasse
	dehydrate	dence	dense
dekaid	decade	denie	deny
delagate	delegate	dentafrice	
delemma			dentifrice
	dilemma		

Incorrect	Correct	Incorrect	Correct
dentel	dental	descriminate	discriminate
dentice	dentist	desease	disease
denyal	denial	Desember	December
deoderant	deodorant	desent	decent
depature	departure	desicion	decision
dependant	dependent	desicrate	desecrate
dependible	dependable	desided	decided
depervation	depravation	desifer	decipher
depo	depot	desine	design
depravashun	deprivation	desireable	desirable
depresent	depressant	desolit	desolate
depricate	deprecate	desparate	desperate
deprieve	deprive	despare	despair
deps	depths	desprit	desperate
depudy	deputy	dessertion	desertion
derick	derrick	dessicate	desiccate
derileck	derelict	dessmal	decimal
derje	dirge	destenation	destination
desabl	decibel	destribute	distribute
desastrous	disastrous	det	debt
descover	discover	detale	detail
descrepancy	discrepancy	deteck	detect
		deteriate	deteriorate

Incorrect	Correct	Incorrect	Correct
detestible		dier	dire
	detestable	diference	
detterent			difference
	deterrent	difftheria	
dettergent			diphtheria
	detergent	dificult	difficult
dettermine		difrenshal	
	determine		differential
devel	devil	difuse	diffuse
devellop	develop	digestable	
devert	divert		digestible
devide	divide	diging	digging
devine	divine	digresive	
devistate			digressive
	devastate	dijest	digest
devius	devious	dijitallus	digitalis
devorce	divorce	dilect	dialect
devulge	divulge	diktionery	
dexterous			dictionary
	dextrous	dillema	dilemma
dezign	design	dilligent	diligent
dezil	diesel	dillute	dilute
diacese	diocese	dilusion	delusion
diafram		dimensha precox —	
	diaphragm		dementia praecox
diatishn	dietitian	dimminative	
dicesion	decision		diminutive
dicline	decline	dimolish	
dicshonery			demolish
	dictionary	dimond	diamond
diebetes	diabetes	dinamic	dynamic
dieing	dying	dinate	dinette

Incorrect	Correct	Incorrect	Correct
diner	dinner	discod	discard
dinning	dining	discomodity	
dint	didn't		discommodity
diper	diaper	disconsilite	
dipleat	deplete		disconsolate
diplete	deplete	disconsurt	
diplomer	diploma		disconcert
diposit	deposit	discribe	describe
dirdy	dirty	discrimanate	
direcshon			discriminate
	direction	discription	
dirive	derive		description
dirogative		discurtius	
	derogative		discourteous
diry	diary	discus	discuss
disadent		discwalafy	
	dissident		disqualify
disagrement		disdane	disdain
	disagreement	disect	dissect
disallusion		disegragate	
	disillusion		desegregate
disalow	disallow	disemenate	
disanent			disseminate
	dissonant	disent	dissent
disapate	dissipate	disertion	
disaprobashon			desertion
	disapprobation	disgize	disguise
disaray	disarray	disiduos	
disasterous			deciduous
	disastrous	disign	design
disatisfy	dissatisfy	disimalar	
disbersment			dissimilar
	disbursement		

Incorrect	Correct	Incorrect	Correct
disipal	disciple	dispurse	disperse
disispline		disqualafy	
	discipline		disqualify
disirable		disrepitible	
	desirable		disreputable
dismantel		disrup	disrupt
	dismantle	dissapoint	
dismis	dismiss		disappoint
dismissel		dissappear	
	dismissal		disappear
disociate		dissastrous	
	dissociate		disastrous
disolution		disscount	
	dissolution		discount
disolve	dissolve	disscover	discover
disonest		disscusion	
	dishonest		discussion
dispair	despair	dissern	discern
disparije		dissipline	
	disparage		discipline
dispensery		disspute	dispute
	dispensary	distaf	distaff
disperporshin		distastful	
	disproportion		distasteful
dispicible		distence	distance
	despicable	disterb	disturb
displacment		distilation	
	displacement		distillation
disposess		distingwish	
	dispossess		distinguish
disposible		distint	distinct
	disposable	distraut	
disposil	disposal		distraught

40

Incorrect	Correct	Incorrect	Correct
distres	distress	dominyon	
districk	district		dominion
distroy	destroy	domono	domino
distruction		doner	donor
	destruction	dongaree	
disuade	dissuade		dungaree
dito	ditto	donky	donkey
divaden	dividend	dont	don't
divice	device	donut	doughnut
divise	devise	dooty	duty
divoid	devoid	dor	door
divoshin	devotion	dorible	durable
divurje	diverge	dormatory	
dizease	disease		dormitory
docter	doctor	dormint	dormant
doctrinare		dosege	dosage
	doctrinaire	dosile	docile
docuementery		doudy	dowdy
	documentary	doue	dough
dodel	dawdle	dourger	dowager
dofin	dauphin	dout	doubt
doge	dodge	dovtale	dovetail
dogeral	doggerel	dowery	dowry
doledrums		dragen	dragon
	doldrums	dramer	drama
dolfin	dolphin	dranege	drainage
doller	dollar	draun	drawn
domanere		dred	dread
	domineer	dreem	dream
domasile		drege	dredge
	domicile	drery	dreary
dominent		dres	dress
	dominant	drie	dry

Incorrect	Correct	Incorrect	Correct
drifwood — driftwood		dum — dumb	
dril — drill		dume — doom	
dring — drink		dungin — dungeon	
drivin — drive-in		dunse — dunce	
drivway — driveway		dupleks — duplex	
drizel — drizzle		duplisity — duplicity	
drol — droll		dupplicate — duplicate	
dromendery — dromedary		durration — duration	
droping — dropping		durres — duress	
droup — droop		durring — during	
drouze — drowse		duse — deuce	
drownded — drowned		dutyful — dutiful	
drugery — drudgery		duve — dove	
drugist — druggist		duz — does	
drunkeness — drunkenness		duzen — dozen	
dryd — dried		dwarve — dwarf	
dubbel — double		dy — die	
dubbius — dubious		dyagnose — diagnose	
Duch — Dutch		dycotomy — dichotomy	
duely — duly		dyitery — dietary	
dule — dual		dynasor — dinosaur	
dulness — dullness		dyvon — divan	
dulsit — dulcet			

Incorrect	Correct	Incorrect	Correct
elbo	elbow	embarassed	embarrassed
eleck	elect	embasador	ambassador
eleet	elite	embelish	embellish
elefent	elephant	embezle	embezzle
elegable	eligible	emblim	emblem
elektristy	electricity	embomb	embalm
elfs	elves	embos	emboss
elikser	elixir	embrase	embrace
elipse	ellipse	embrio	embryo
ellaberate	elaborate	embroyder	embroider
ellaquent	eloquent	emfasis	emphasis
ellementary	elementary	eminate	emanate
elliminated	eliminate	emisary	emissary
ellisit	elicit	emity	enmity
ellude	elude	emmergancy	emergency
elluminate	illuminate	emmployee	employee
ellusadate	elucidate	emolient	emollient
...ls	else	emoshun	emotion
...lum	elm	empier	empire
...lve	elf	emporer	emperor
...magrint	emigrant	emptyness	emptiness
...manense	eminence	emty	empty
...narald	emerald	enamerd	enamored

46

Look-Alikes or Sound-Alikes

dairy (food) · diary (personal record)

dam (water) · damn (curse)

Dane (nationality) · deign (deem worthy)

days (plural of day) · daze (confused)

dear (loved) · deer (animal)

debauch (to seduce) · debouch (to march out)

debouch (to march out) · debauch (to seduce)

deceased (dead) · diseased (sick)

decent (good) · descent (go down) · dissent (disagreement)

decree (law) · degree (award from school)

defer (postpone) · differ (disagree)

definite (precise) · definitive (final)

definitive (final) · definite (precise)

defused (without a fuse) · diffused (filtered or mixed in)

deign (deem worthy) · Dane (nationality)

dependence (reliance on others) · dependents (those supported by a given person)

dependents (those supported by a given person) · dependence (reliance on others)

depositary (the one receiving a deposit) · depository (a place where anything is deposited)

deposition (testimony in writing) · disposition (temperament)

depository (a place where anything is deposited) · depositary (the one receiving a deposit)

depraved (evil) · deprived (forbidden)

deprecate (express disapproval) · depreciate (to lessen in value)

depreciate (to lessen in value) · deprecate (express disapproval)

descendant (has all the meanings of descendent *plus* functions as a noun, and means *offspring*) · descendent (falling; proceeding from an original ancestor)

descendent (falling; proceeding from an original ancestor) · descendant (has all the meanings of descendent *plus* functions as noun, and means *offspring*)

descent (go down) · dissent (disagreement) · decent (good)

desert (dry land) · dessert (food)

desolate (barren) · dissolute (given to wasteful, pleasure-seeking activities)

dessert (food) · desert (dry land)

detract (to take away from) · distract (to divert)

deuce (two) · Duce (Mussolini)

device (a scheme, means) · devise (invent)

dew (moisture) · do (to act) · due (owed)

diagram (sketch) · diaphragm (part of body)

diary (personal record) · dairy (food)

die (death) · dye (change color)

differ (disagree) · defer (postpone)

diffused (filtered or mixed in) · defused (without a fuse)

43

dinar (Yugoslav currency) ·
dinner (meal)

dine (eat) · dyne (a unit of
force in physics)

dinner (meal) · dinar
(Yugoslav currency)

disapprove (condemn) ·
disprove (prove wrong)

disburse (pay out) · disperse
(break up)

discomfit (to upset another)
· discomfort (uneasiness)

discomfort (uneasiness) ·
discomfit (to upset another)

discreet (prudent) · discrete
(separate, disconnected)

discrete (separate,
disconnected) · discreet
(prudent)

diseased (sick) · deceased
(dead)

disposition (temperament) ·
deposition (testimony in
writing)

dissent (disagreement) ·
decent (good) · descent (go
down)

dissolute (given to wasteful,
pleasure-seeking activities) ·
desolate (barren)

distract (to divert) · detract
(to take away from)

divers (several) · diverse
(different)

diverse (different) · divers
(several)

do (to act) · due (owed) ·
dew (moisture)

doe (deer) · dough (bread)

does (female deers) · doze
(nap)

done (finished) · dun (ask for
payment)

dual (two) · duel (fight)

dudgeon (anger; resentment)
· dungeon (cell in basement
of a prison)

dye (change color) · die
(death)

dyeing (changing color) ·
dying (death)

dyne (a unit of force in
physics) · dine (eat)

E

Incorrect	Correct	Incorrect	Co
earing	earring	efishency	
earlyer	earlier		— effici
easly	easily	eg	
easment		ege	e
	— easement	eger	ea
ebiny	ebony	eggsecutive	
ebulient	ebullient		— execu
ecconomic		egle	e
	— economic	egoe	
ech	etch	egsack	e
eclesiestical		egsactly	exa
	— ecclesiastical	egstempiraneus	
eclips	eclipse		— extemporan
eco	echo	egstink	e
economacal		egzert	
	— economical	egzotic	
edable	edible	eighteen	
edipus	Oedipus		— ei
editer	editor	ejeck	
educatable		eksalt	
	— educable	eksclud	
edyucate	educate	ekscrewshiat	
eele	eel		— ex
eether	either	eksist	
efect	effect	ekstacy	
efervesent		ekzonerate	
	— effervescent		
effert	effort	elagent	
eficashus		elagie	
	— efficacious	element	

Incorrect	Correct	Incorrect	Correct
enamy	enemy	entier	entire
encompes		entise	entice
	encompass	entree	entry
encorporate		entreet	entreat
	incorporate	entreprise	
endere	endear		enterprise
endever	endeavor	enuf	enough
endoctrinate		enunsiate	
	indoctrinate		enunciate
endorsment		envelup	envelop
	endorsement	envie	envy
enfiltrate		envirement	
	infiltrate		environment
enforcible		envius	envious
	enforceable	envoke	invoke
engeneer		envyable	enviable
	engineer	envys	envies
Englind	England	epacure	epicure
enigetic	energetic	epademic	
enivate	enervate		epidemic
enny	any	epasod	episode
enoble	ennoble	epataf	epitaph
enraige	enrage	eppick	epic
enrap	enwrap	eppok	epoch
enrapcher		equalibrium	
	enrapture		equilibrium
ensin	ensign	equaly	equally
entale	entail	equanocks	
entamology			equinox
	entomology	equidy	equity
entatain	entertain	equipt	equipped
enterance		equivilent	
	entrance		equivalent

47

Incorrect	Correct	Incorrect	Correct
erace	erase	eves	eaves
eratic	erratic	evning	evening
erb	herb	evry	every
erektion	erection	evrywear	everywhere
erind	errand	evul	evil
erl	earl	exackly	exactly
erly	early	exacuate	execute
ermin	ermine	exagarate	exaggerate
ernest	earnest	examanation	examination
eroneus	erroneous	exaust	exhaust
eror	error	excede	exceed
erth	earth	excell	excel
Ery	Erie	excentric	eccentric
eryudite	erudite	excercise	exercise
esay	essay	excitment	excitement
escourt	escort	exessive	excessive
esculator	escalator	exest	exist
esential	essential	exgurshin	excursion
Eskamo	Eskimo	exhail	exhale
espianoge	espionage	exhorbitant	exorbitant
estamate	estimate	exibit	exhibit
Ester	Easter	existance	existence
et	ate	exitus	exodus
eternaty	eternity	expell	expel
ethacal	ethical		
etikete	etiquette		
evalushun	evolution		
evedence	evidence		

Incorrect	Correct	Incorrect	Correct
expence	**expense**	exsize	**excise**
expendible		exspense	**expense**
	expendable	exsperience	
experashun			**experience**
	expiration	extention	
experiance			**extension**
	experience	extracate	
explaination			**extricate**
	explanation	extracuricular	
explative			**extracurricular**
	expletive	extravert	
explisit	**explicit**		**extrovert**
exposel	**exposal**	extravigent	
expres	**express**		**extravagant**
exray	**x-ray**	extreem	**extreme**
exsecutive		extrordinary	
	executive		**extraordinary**
exseed	**exceed**	exzema	**eczema**
exsellent		exzile	**exile**
	excellent	exzilirate	
exsept	**except**		**exhilarate**
exsessive		Eyetalian	**Italian**
	excessive	eyether	**either**
exsist	**exist**	ezy	**easy**
exsiteable		ezzampel	
	excitable		**example**

Look-Alikes or Sound-Alikes

earn (gain) · **urn** (vase)

eccentric (strange) · **acentric** (not centered)

edible (eatable) · **addible** (can be added)

edition (publishing) · **addition** (anything added)

e'er (ever) · **air** (atmosphere) · **heir** (one who inherits)

eerie (ghostly) · **Erie** (the lake) · **eery** (eerie) · **aerie** (eagle's nest)

eery (eerie) · **eerie** (ghostly) · **Erie** (the lake) · **aerie** (eagle's nest)

effect (result; to bring about) · **affect** (to cause)

effective (impressive; operative) · **affective** (emotional)

egret (heron) · **aigrette** (ornamental plume)

eight (the number) · **ate** (did eat)

either (one of two) · **ether** (drug)

elder (refers to age and wisdom gained) · **older** (refers to age only)

elegy (poem, lament) · **eulogy** (praise)

elicit (draw out) · **illicit** (illegal)

elude (evade) · **illude** (cheat) · **allude** (refer to)

elusion (evasion, escape by deception) · **allusion** (reference to) · **illusion** (false impression)

elusive (evasive) · **allusive** (referring to) · **illusive** (deceptive)

emend (remove errors) · **amend** (change)

emerge (to come out) · **immerge** (to plunge into)

emersed (standing above) · **immersed** (plunged in liquid)

emigrant (leaves country) · **immigrant** (enters country)

eminent (well-known) · **imminent** (about to happen)

emit (to send out) · **immit** (to send in)

emollient (softening) · **emolument** (profit, salary, fee)

emolument (profit, salary, fee) · **emollient** (softening)

empire (dominion) · **umpire** (referee)

enable (to make able) · **unable** (not able)

enervate (to deprive of nerve or strength) · **innervate** (to invigorate)

enmity (hostility) · **amity** (friendship)

ensure (to make sure or secure) · **insure** (an alternate spelling of ensure)

entomology (study of insects) · **etymology** (study of words)

envelop (to surround) · **envelope** (stationery)

epic (classic) · **epoch** (age)

epigraph (motto) · **epitaph** (inscription) · **epithet** (curse)

equable (not varying) · **equitable** (fair)

equitable (fair) · **equable** (not varying)

era (age) · **error** (mistake)

ere (before) · **err** (to do wrong)

erect (to build) · **eruct** (to belch, or cast forth)

Erie (the lake) · **eerie** (ghostly) · **eery** (eerie) · **aerie** (eagle's nest)

erotic (sexy) · **erratic** (uneven)

errand (trip) · **errant** (roving)

50

eruct (to belch, or cast forth) · **erect** (to build)

eruption (a bursting out) · **irruption** (a bursting in)

especial (exceptional, preeminent) · **special** (particular, specific)

essay (composition) · **assay** (evaluate)

estray (noun, anything out of its normal place) · **astray** (adv., out of the right place)

ether (drug) · **either** (one of two)

etymology (study of words) · **entomology** (study of insects)

eunuch (sexless) · **unique** (sole)

everyone (all persons) · **every one** (each one, considered separately, one after the other)

everything (the entire situation, viewed as one total mass) · **every thing** (each item in the given situation)

ewe (sheep) · **yew** (tree) · **you** (person)

exalt (glorify) · **exult** (rejoice)

exceed (go beyond) · **accede** (agree)

except (leave out) · **accept** (agree)

exceptionable (objectionable) · **exceptional** (out of the ordinary)

exceptional (out of the ordinary) · **exceptionable** (objectionable)

excess (too much) · **access** (get to)

exercise (practice) · **exorcise** (drive away evil spirits)

expansive (capable of stretching) · **expensive** (costly)

expensive (costly) · **expansive** (capable of stretching)

expose (to uncover) · **exposé** (an account of scandalous facts or shameful deeds)

exposé (an account of scandalous facts or shameful deeds) · **expose** (to uncover)

extant (still done) · **extent** (width)

eye (see) · **aye** (yes) · **I** (me)

F

Incorrect	Correct	Incorrect	Correct
fabel	fable	famin	famine
fabrik	fabric	famly	family
fabulus	fabulous	famus	famous
faceing	facing	fancyful	fanciful
fachewal	factual	fansy	fancy
fachuos	fatuous	fanticy	fantasy
facinate	fascinate	fantom	phantom
facshun	faction	farely	fairly
facter	factor	farenheit	
factery	factory		Fahrenheit
fadelity	fidelity	farmacy	
faent	faint		pharmacy
faery	fairy	farse	farce
faim	fame	fase	face
fain	feign	fasetious	
faksimile			facetious
	facsimile	fashial	facial
fakt	fact	fashon	fashion
fakulty	faculty	fasilitate	
fale	fail		facilitate
falibel	fallible	fasinate	fascinate
falicitate		fasithia	forsythia
	felicitate	fasodd	façade
falicy	fallacy	fassen	fasten
falkin	falcon	fateeg	fatigue
fallse	false	fatel	fatal
falsafy	falsify	faten	fatten
falseto	falsetto	fatful	fateful
falt	fault	fath	faith
familliar	familiar	father	farther

52

Incorrect	Correct	Incorrect	Correct
fathim	fathom	fergive	forgive
faught	fought	fernish	furnish
faverible		fersake	forsake
	favorable	fertil	fertile
fawcet	faucet	fery	ferry
fawl	fall	fesable	feasible
fayth	faith	festavil	festival
feal	feel	feter	fetter
feasco	fiasco	fether	feather
Febuary		feu	few
	February	feuneril	funeral
fech	fetch	feurius	furious
fedral	federal	feva	fever
feeblely	feebly	ficks	fix
feend	fiend	fidle	fiddle
feest	feast	fiebrus	fibrous
feeture	feature	fiel	file
feild	field	fier	fire
feirce	fierce	figet	fidget
fel	fell	figger	figure
fella	fellow	fikil	fickle
feller	fellow	Filadelphia	
fellony	felony		Philadelphia
fellt	felt	filanderer	
femenine			philanderer
	feminine	filanthropy	
fenobarbital			philanthropy
	phenobarbital	filately	philately
fenomenon		filay	filet
	phenomenon	file	faille
fense	fence	filharmonic	
fere	fear		philharmonic
ferget	forget	fillter	filter

53

Incorrect	Correct	Incorrect	Correct
fillum	film	flamible	
filmsy	flimsy		flammable
filosophy		flaper	flapper
	philosophy	flasid	flaccid
finanse	finance	flatary	flattery
finanshil		flaten	flatten
	financial	flater	flatter
finatic	fanatic	flaver	flavor
finese	finesse	flaygrent	flagrant
fingger	finger	flech	flesh
finil	final	flecksible	flexible
finly	finely	flee	flea
fireing	firing	fleese	fleece
firey	fiery	flegeling	
firlo	furlough		fledgling
firment	ferment	flem	phlegm
firoshus	ferocious	flert	flirt
firther	further	flete	fleet
fishion	fission	flie	fly
fisically		flikker	flicker
	physically	flipint	flippant
fisiology		flirtacious	
	physiology		flirtatious
fite	fight	flite	flight
fiting	fitting	flok	flock
fium	fume	floorist	florist
flabergas		floot	flute
	flabbergast	flor	flaw
flache	flake	flore	floor
flachulent		floresent	
	flatulent		fluorescent
flaging	flagging	floride	fluoride
flaim	flame	floris	florist

Incorrect	Correct	Incorrect	Correct
floriscope	fluoroscope	fondal	fondle
florish	flourish	fonetic	phonetic
Florrida	Florida	fonics	phonics
flote	float	fonograph	phonograph
flotila	flotilla	fonte	font
flouer	flower	fony	phony
floun	flown	forcast	forecast
flownder	flounder	forceable	forcible
flownse	flounce	forchoon	fortune
flud	flood	forck	fork
flued	fluid	forclose	foreclose
fluint	fluent	forebid	forbid
flys	flies	fored	forehead
fo	foe	fore ever	forever
fobia	phobia	forfit	forfeit
focit	faucet	forgone	foregone
focks	fox	forgry	forgery
fogy	foggy	forhead	forehead
foke	folk	forin	foreign
fokil	focal	forje	forge
fokis	focus	formadable	formidable
foksel	forecastle	formaly	formally
foled	fold	forman	foreman
folige	foliage	forment	foment
foller	follow	formil	formal
foly	folly	formost	foremost
fom	farm	forrest	forest
fome	foam	forrum	forum
fomer	former	forsee	foresee
fomula	formula	forsight	foresight
fon	fawn	fortatude	fortitude

Incorrect	Correct	Incorrect	Correct
forteen	fourteen	frojalent	fraudulent
fosfate	phosphate	frok	frock
fosforescence	phosphorescence	fronteersman	frontiersman
fosforus	phosphorus	frontspiece	frontispiece
fosil	fossil	frosen	frozen
foth	forth	frought	fraught
foto	photo	froun	frown
fountin	fountain	frugl	frugal
fourty	forty	fruntil	frontal
foward	forward	frutful	fruitful
fownd	found	Fryday	Friday
fraim	frame	fued	feud
frale	frail	fuedal	feudal
frase	phrase	fugative	fugitive
frate	freight	fuge	fugue
fraygrince	fragrance	fuje	fudge
freek	freak	fullfil	fulfill
Freid	Freud	fumbil	fumble
frekel	freckle	funcshin	function
frend	friend	fundimental	fundamental
frequincy	frequency	funel	funnel
freshin	freshen	funeril	funeral
fricasee	fricassee	fungis	fungus
fricshin	friction	funy	funny
frier	friar	furlow	furlough
frinje	fringe	furm	firm
frite	fright	furnature	furniture
friternel	fraternal		
frivlous	frivolous		

56

Incorrect	Correct	Incorrect	Correct
fury	furry	futball	football
fusalege	fuselage	futere	future
fusha	fuchsia	futil	futile
fust	first	fyancy	fiance

Look-Alikes or Sound-Alikes

facet (side) · **faucet** (water)

facility (skill) · **felicity** (happiness)

faerie (obsolete form of fairy, meaning enchantment) · **fairy** (a supernatural being) · **ferry** (boat)

fair (just) · **fare** (pay for travel)

fairy (a supernatural being) · **faerie** (obsolete form of fairy meaning enchantment) · **ferry** (boat)

faker (fraud) · **fakir** (Moslem sect)

fantasy (a far-fetched imaginary idea) · **phantasy** (same as *fantasy*, more archaic)

farther (refers to physical distance) · **further** (refers to extent or degree)

fatal (deathly) · **fateful** (of very great importance)

fate (destiny) · **fete** (festival)

fateful (of very great importance) · **fatal** (deathly)

faun (rural deity) · **fawn** (servile; young deer)

faze (worry) · **phase** (stage) · **fays** (fairies)

feint (pretend) · **faint** (weak)

felicity (happiness) · **facility** (skill)

ferment (yeast) · **foment** (incite)

fiancé (engaged) · **finance** (money)

fiend (monster) · **friend** (companion)

filing (put in order) · **filling** (to make full)

finale (the end) · **finally** (at last) · **finely** (excellently)

find (locate) · **fined** (penalty)

fineness (being fine) · **finesse** (subtle; skill)

fir (tree) · **fur** (hair of animal)

fiscal (money) · **physical** (body)

fisher (one who fishes) · **fissure** (split)

flagrant (glaring) · **fragrant** (nice odor)

flair (aptitude) · **flare** (burn)

flaunt (ostentatious display) · **flout** (reject contemptuously)

flea (insect) · **flee** (run away)

flèche (a spire) · **flesh** (meat)

flesh (meat) · **flèche** (a spire)

flew (did fly) · **flu** (influenza) · **flue** (chimney)

flour (food) · **flower** (plant)

flout (reject contemptuously) · **flaunt** (ostentatious display)

fogy (conservative) · **foggy** (blurred)

foment (incite) · **ferment** (yeast)

fondling (caressing) · **foundling** (deserted infant)

57

for (in behalf of) · **four** (number) · **fore** (golf)

forego (precede) · **forgo** (do without)

foreword (introduction) · **forward** (move ahead)

formally (conventionally) · **formerly** (before now)

fort (military) · **forte** (strong point)

forth (forward) · **fourth** (number)

foul (dirty, unfair) · **fowl** (bird)

foundling (deserted infant) · **fondling** (caressing)

franc (French money) · **frank** (blunt)

Frances (girl) · **Francis** (boy) · **France's** (of France)

frays (battles) · **phrase** (words)

frees (set free) · **freeze** (cold)

frenetic (frantic) · **phrenetic** (insane)

friend (companion) · **fiend** (monster)

funeral (a ceremony for the dead) · **funereal** (mournful)

funereal (mournful) · **funeral** (a ceremony for the dead)

Fuehrer (leader used esp. for Adolf Hitler) · **furor** (commotion)

fur (hair of animal) · **fir** (tree)

furor (commotion) · **Fuehrer** (leader used esp. for Adolf Hitler)

further (refers to extent or degree) · **farther** (refers to physical distance)

58

G

Incorrect	Correct	Incorrect	Correct
gaberdeen	——	gaskit	gasket
	gabardine	gasseous	gaseous
gaget	gadget	gastly	ghastly
gail	gale	gatare	guitar
gailic	gallic	gawdy	gaudy
gaim	game	gawse	gauze
galacksy	galaxy	gaz	gas
galary	gallery	gazel	gazelle
galent	gallant	gazet	gazette
galin	gallon	geep	jeep
galip	gallop	geer	gear
galows	gallows	geesha	geisha
gama globlin	——	geetar	guitar
	gamma globulin	geneology	——
gambul	gamble		genealogy
gammit	gamut	genrally	——
gangreen	——		generally
	gangrene	genrus	generous
garantee	——	gentelman	——
	guarantee		gentleman
gararge	garage	gentlely	gently
garbige	garbage	genuwine	——
gard	guard		genuine
gardin	garden	genyus	genius
gardner	gardener	gergul	gurgle
garilus	garrulous	gerl	girl
garit	garret	germain	germane
garlick	garlic	Germin	German
gasalene	gasoline	gescher	gesture
gasha	geisha	gess	guess

59

Incorrect	Correct	Incorrect	Correct
gest	guest	gliserin	glycerin
getto	ghetto	gliter	glitter
gidance	guidance	globle	global
gide	guide	glorafy	glorify
gidy	giddy	glosary	glossary
gient	giant	glume	gloom
gigal	giggle	glutin	glutton
giggolo	gigolo	goble	gobble
gilless	guileless	goblit	goblet
gimick	gimmick	goch	gauche
giminasium	gymnasium	gode	goad
ginacology	gynecology	godess	goddess
ginee	guinea	gofer	gopher
gingam	gingham	gole	goal
girdal	girdle	gon	gone
gise	guise	gondala	gondola
git	get	gord	gourd
givaway	giveaway	Gorgia	Georgia
		gorgous	gorgeous
giy	guy	gormet	gourmet
glair	glare	gosamer	gossamer
glajer	glazier		
glamerus	glamorous	gosip	gossip
glanse	glance	gosspel	gospel
glas	glass	gost	ghost
glashul	glacial	gote	goat
gleem	gleam	goten	gotten
glidder	glider	goun	gown
glimer	glimmer	govener	governor
glimse	glimpse	govenment	government

60

Incorrect	Correct	Incorrect	Correct
graditude	**gratitude**	greze	**grease**
gradjel	**gradual**	grile	**grille**
graf	**graph**	grimas	**grimace**
graid	**grade**	groap	**grope**
gramer	**grammar**	grone	**groan**
gran	**grand**	groop	**group**
granaid	**grenade**	grose	**gross**
grandaughter		grosry	**grocery**
	— granddaughter	grotesk	
grandur	**grandeur**		**— grotesque**
grane	**grain**	gruje	**grudge**
gras	**grass**	gruvil	**grovel**
grashus	**gracious**	guage	**gauge**
gravaty	**gravity**	gud	**good**
gravle	**gravel**	guidence	
grayhound			**— guidance**
	— greyhound	gullable	**gullible**
graysful	**graceful**	guner	**gunner**
greatful	**grateful**	guse	**goose**
gredy	**greedy**	guter	**gutter**
greif	**grief**	guterul	**guttural**
greive	**grieve**	guverment	
greivence			**— government**
	— grievance	guvnor	**governor**
grene	**green**	guyser	**geyser**
grete	**greet**	gypsim	**gypsum**
grewsome			
	— gruesome		

Look-Alikes or Sound-Alikes

gage (security) · **gauge** (measure)

gait (walk) · **gate** (door)

gallstone (pertains to medicine) · **goldstone** (pertains to mineralogy)

gamble (bet) · **gambol** (frolic)

gamin (a street urchin) · **gammon** (a deceitful trick)

gantlet (narrowing of two railroad tracks; punishment) · **gauntlet** (glove)

gat (obsolete past tense of get) · **ghat** (a pass through a mountain chain)

gauntlet (glove) · **gantlet** (narrowing of two railroad tracks; punishment)

genius (brilliant) · **genus** (class)

genteel (polite) · **gentle** (tame) · **gentile** (any non-Jew)

gesture (move) · **jester** (clown)

ghat (a pass through a mountain chain) · **gat** (obsolete past tense of get)

gibe (to sneer at) · **jibe** (to agree; to swing from side to side)

gild (gold cover) · **guild** (association)

gilt (gold) · **guilt** (lawbreaking)

glacier (iceberg) · **glazier** (glass maker)

gloom (a sad, dismal atmosphere) · **glume** (a botanical term)

glume (a botanical term) · **gloom** (a sad, dismal atmosphere)

gluten (substance found in flour of wheat and other grains) · **glutton** (a person who eats to excess)

glutton (a person who eats to excess) · **gluten** (substance found in flour of wheat and other grains)

gnu (animal) · **knew** (did know) · **new** (not old)

goldstone (pertains to mineralogy) · **gallstone** (pertains to medicine)

gorilla (ape) · **guerrilla** (war)

grate (bars; grind) · **great** (large)

grease (oil or unctuous matter) · **Greece** (a nation in Europe)

grip (grasp) · **gripe** (complain) · **grippe** (disease)

grisly (ghastly) · **gristly** (full of bones) · **grizzly** (grayish)

groan (moan) · **grown** (mature)

guarantee (to secure, insure; used as verb, this is the preferred spelling by lawyers) · **guaranty** (same as guarantee)

guessed (did guess) · **guest** (visitor)

guild (association) · **gild** (gold cover)

guilt (lawbreaker) · **gilt** (gold)

H

Incorrect	Correct	Incorrect	Correct
habadasher —		hamer —	hammer
	— haberdasher	hamlit —	hamlet
habichawate —		handel —	handle
	— habituate	handycap —	
habillitate —			— handicap
	— habilitate	hanful —	handful
hach —	hatch	hangkerchif —	
hadick —	haddock		— handkerchief
hae —	hay	hant —	haunt
haf —	half	hapin —	happen
hagerd —	haggard	happly —	happily
hagil —	haggle	haradin —	harridan
hainus —	heinous	harange —	
hairbrained —			— harangue
	— harebrained	harber —	harbor
hairloom —		harboild —	
	— heirloom		— hardboiled
hait —	hate	hardning —	
hake —	hack		— hardening
halaluyah —		haried —	harried
	— hallelujah	Harlacwin —	
Halaween —			— Harlequin
	— Halloween	harmoenyus —	
halfs —	halves		— harmonious
halow —	hallow	harnis —	harness
halsion —	halcyon	harrass —	harass
halusinate —		harth —	hearth
	— hallucinate	harty —	hearty
hamberger —		hasard —	hazard
	— hamburger	hasen —	hasten

Incorrect	Correct	Incorrect	Correct
hasienda — hacienda		hellmit — helmet	
hasle — hassle		helo — hello	
hatchit — hatchet		helth — health	
Hawayi — Hawaii		hemaglobin — hemoglobin	
hawse — horse		hemesphere — hemisphere	
hiyena — hyena		hemmorage — hemorrhage	
haylo — halo		hena — henna	
hayrim — harem		hensfourth — henceforth	
hayvin — haven		heratige — heritage	
hazil — hazel		herbashus — herbaceous	
headake — headache		herdel — hurdle	
headinist — hedonist		herild — herald	
headress — headdress		hering — herring	
heartally — heartily		herisy — heresy	
hecktic — hectic		herl — hurl	
hed — head		hermatige — hermitage	
hede — heed		heros — heroes	
heep — heap		herredity — heredity	
heet — heat		herron — heron	
heffer — heifer		her's — hers	
heighth — height		herse — hearse	
heirarchy — hierarchy		hertofore — heretofore	
heje — hedge		hesatate — hesitate	
hekil — heckle		hetagenius — heterogeneous	
heksigon — hexagon			
hel — hell			
hellicopter — helicopter			

Incorrect	Correct	Incorrect	Correct
hethin	heathen	hipnotist	
heve	heave		hypnotist
heven	heaven	hipocrite	
hevy	heavy		hypocrite
hibonate		hipopotimis	
	hibernate		hippopotamus
hibread	hybrid	hirarchy	
hibrow	highbrow		hierarchy
hich	hitch	hirling	hireling
hiden	hidden	hiroglific	
hideus	hideous		hieroglyphic
hidrafobia		histeria	hysteria
	hydrophobia	histry	history
hidranja		hoby	hobby
	hydrangea	hocky	hockey
hidraulic		hojpoj	
	hydraulic		hodgepodge
hidrint	hydrant	hoks	hoax
hidrogen		holesale	wholesale
	hydrogen	holesome	
hiensite	hindsight		wholesome
hifen	hyphen	holindaze	
hight	height		hollandaise
hikery	hickory	hollicust	
hillarius	hilarious		holocaust
hinderance		holliday	holiday
	hindrance	holow	hollow
hiness	highness	holyness	holiness
hinj	hinge	hom	home
hipadermic		homaker	
	hypodermic		homemaker
hipertension		homaside	
	hypertension		homicide

Incorrect	Correct	Incorrect	Correct
homegeneous —		horty —	haughty
	— homogeneous	hosh —	harsh
homly —	homely	hospatol —	hospital
hommage —		hostige —	hostage
	— homage	hostle —	hostile
homsted —		hottel —	hotel
	— homestead	houshold —	
honerable —			— household
	— honorable	houswife —	
honeydo —			— housewife
	— honeydew	houzing —	housing
honist —	honest	hovist —	harvest
honny —	honey	howel —	howl
honrary —	honorary	hownd —	hound
hont —	haunt	howzes —	houses
hoo —	who	hoy polloy —	
hoove —	hoof		— hoi polloi
hopeing —	hoping	hoyst —	hoist
horafyd —	horrified	hoze —	hose
horemone —		hoziery —	hosiery
	— hormone	hud —	hood
horenjus —		hudel —	huddle
	— horrendous	huf —	hoof
horible —	horrible	huk —	hook
horizen —	horizon	hukelbery —	
hornit —	hornet		— huckleberry
horra —	horror	humer —	humor
horrorscope —		humilliate —	
	— horoscope		— humiliate
horsey —	horsy	huming —	humming
horspital —	hospital	humrus —	
hortaculcher —			— humorous
	— horticulture	hunderd —	hundred

66

Incorrect	**Correct**	Incorrect	**Correct**
hungar	**hunger**	hyatis	**hiatus**
hungary	**hungry**	hygene	**hygiene**
huray	**hurray**	hymnil	**hymnal**
huricane		hypacrite	
	— hurricane		**— hypocrite**
husle	**hustle**	hypatheticle	
huvel	**hovel**		**— hypothetical**
huver	**hover**	hypocracy	
huzbind	**— husband**		**— hypocrisy**
huzy	**hussy**		

Look-Alikes or Sound-Alikes

hail (salute; ice) · **hale** (hearty)

hair (on head) · **hare** (rabbit)

haircut (the process of cutting the hair) · **haricot** (bean; stew)

hale (hearty) · **hail** (salute; ice)

hall (room) · **haul** (pull in)

hallow (to make holy) · **halo** (circle of light around head to show saintliness) · **hollow** (empty inside) · **holler** (to shout)

handsome (looks) · **hansom** (cab)

hangar (shelter) · **hanger** (clothes holder)

haricot (bean; stew) · **haircut** (the process of cutting the hair)

hart (stag) · **heart** (body)

haunch (buttocks) · **hunch** (a guess, conjecture)

hay (dried grass eaten by cattle) · **hey!** (an exclamation)

heal (mend) · **heel** (of foot) · **he'll** (he will)

hear (with the ear) · **here** (this place)

heard (did hear) · **herd** (animals)

heaume (helmet) · **home** (a house)

heir (inheritor) · **air** (atmosphere) · **e'er** (ever)

hence (from this time or place) · **thence** (from that time or place)

heroin (drug) · **heroine** (lady hero)

hew (chop) · **hue** (color) · **Hugh** (name)

hey! (an exclamation) · **hay** (dried grass eaten by cattle)

higher (taller) · **hire** (employ)

him (he) · **hymn** (song)

hoard (collect) · **horde** (swarm)

hoarse (harsh) · **horse** (animal)

hoes (digs) · hose (stockings)

hole (opening) · whole (complete)

holey (having holes) · holy (religious) · wholly (fully)

holiday (a day of exemption from work) · holy day (a religious feast day)

holler (to shout) · hollow (empty inside) · hallow (to make holy) · halo (circle of light around head to show saintliness)

hollow (empty inside) · hallow (to make holy) · halo (circle of light around head to show saintliness) · holler (to shout)

holy day (a religious feast day) · holiday (a day of exemption from work)

home (a house) · heaume (helmet)

homogeneous (of the same character, essentially alike) · homogenous (of common origin)

homogenous (of common origin) · homogeneous (of the same character, essentially alike)

hoop (circle) · whoop (holler)

hospitable (friendly) · hospital (for the sick)

hour (time) · our (belongs to us)

hue (color) · hew (chop) · Hugh (name)

human (of man) · humane (kind)

hunch (a guess, conjecture) · haunch (buttocks)

hymn (song) · him (he)

hypercritical (over-critical) · hypocritical (pretending to be what one is not)

I

Incorrect	Correct	Incorrect	Correct
iadine	iodine	iland	island
ibeks	ibex	ile	isle
iceing	icing	ilegal	illegal
ich	itch	ilegible	illegible
ideel	ideal	Ilinois	Illinois
ideer	idea	iliterate	illiterate
idendicle	identical	illagitimate	
identafy	identify		illegitimate
idget	idiot	illiad	Iliad
idiet	idiot	illisit	illicit
idiology	ideology	ilness	illness
idiosyncracy		ilogigal	illogical
	idiosyncrasy	ilujun	illusion
idium	idiom	iluminate	
idollater	idolater		illuminate
idylic	idyllic	ilustrate	illustrate
idz	ides	imaculate	
iern	iron		immaculate
ignamineus		imadgine	
	ignominious		imagine
ignerant	ignorant	imaginible	
ignor	ignore		imaginable
igwana	iguana	imagrint	
igzasprate			immigrant
	exasperate	imatation	
ikon	icon		imitation
ikonaclass		imaterial	
	iconoclast		immaterial
ikthiology		imature	
	ichthyology		immature

69

Incorrect	Correct	Incorrect	Correct
imbicile —	**imbecile**	impell ——	**impel**
imbiew ——	**imbue**	impenitrible	
imeasureable			**— impenetrable**
	— immeasurable	impetent	
imediate			**— impotent**
	— immediate	impicunius	
imense —	**immense**		**— impecunious**
imige ——	**image**	impinje —	**impinge**
iminint —	**imminent**	impius —	**impious**
immagination		implament	
	— imagination		**— implement**
immemrable		implaquable	
	— immemorable		**— implacable**
immesh —	**enmesh**	implie ——	**imply**
imobil —	**immobile**	implisit —	**implicit**
imoral —	**immoral**	imployee	
imortil —	**immortal**		**— employee**
impare ——	**impair**	inpolite —	**impolite**
imparshal—	**impartial**	importence	
impashent			**— importance**
	— impatient	imposibility	
impashoned			**— impossibility**
	— impassioned	imprasario	
impass —	**impasse**		**— impresario**
impaterbable		impres —	**impress**
	— imperturbable	impreshin	
impatus —	**impetus**		**— impression**
impech —	**impeach**	impromtu	
impecible			**— impromptu**
	— impeccable	improvment	
impeed ——	**impede**		**— improvement**
impeerial		impuin —	**impugn**
	— imperial	impyaty —	**impiety**

Incorrect	Correct	Incorrect	Correct
imune	immune	incombent	
inable	enable		incumbent
inabt	inapt	incondecent	
inacceptable			incandescent
	unacceptable	incorijible	
inain	inane		incorrigible
inate	innate	incorperate	
inaugarate			incorporate
	inaugurate	incourage	
inavoidable			encourage
	unavoidable	incrament	
inbalance			increment
	imbalance	incredable	
inbieb	imbibe		incredible
incalcable		increse	increase
	incalculable	incroch	encroach
incarnit	incarnate	incured	incurred
incesint	incessant	incuring	
inchant	enchant		incurring
inchoir	enquire	incyclopedia	
incidently			encyclopedia
	incidentally	indago	indigo
incipid	insipid	indalent	indolent
inclanation		indefensable	
	inclination		indefensible
inclemit		indekerus	
	inclement		indecorous
inclood	include	indeks	index
inclosher		indelable	
	enclosure		indelible
incogneto		independant	
	incognito		independent

Incorrect	Correct	Incorrect	Correct
indesent	indecent	inersha	inertia
indesirable		inervate	
	undesirable		innervate
indetted	indebted	inevatable	
indiferent			inevitable
	indifferent	inexrable	
indijinus			inexorable
	indigenous	infadelaty	
indiketive			infidelity
	indicative	infalible	
inditement			infallible
	indictment	infanitly	infinitely
individuly		infecshun	
	individually		infection
indocternate		infent	infant
	indoctrinate	infered	infrared
indomnitable		inferier	inferior
	indomitable	infermary	
indowment			infirmary
	endowment	infermashun	
inducment			information
	inducement	infimous	
indurance			infamous
	endurance	infinative	
industral			infinitive
	industrial	infincy	infancy
Indyan	Indian	infiriate	infuriate
inefable		inflamable	
	ineffable		inflammable
ineficashus		inflashin	inflation
	inefficacious	infleckshun	
iner	inner		inflection

72

Incorrect	Correct	Incorrect	Correct
influinse	**influence**	inlighten	
inforce	**enforce**		**— enlighten**
infrence		innacurate	
	— inference		**—inaccurate**
infur	**infer**	innapropriate	
infuze	**infuse**		**— inappropriate**
ingagement		innaugurate	
	— engagement		**— inaugurate**
ingection		innauspicious	
	— injection		**— inauspicious**
ingine	**engine**	innebreate	
Inglish	**English**		**— inebriate**
ingrachiate		innechative	
	— ingratiate		**— initiative**
ingrave	**engrave**	inneficient	
ingreedient			**— inefficient**
	— ingredient	innoculate	
inhabatint			**— inoculate**
	— inhabitant	inocense	
inhabition			**— innocence**
	— inhibition	inocuous	
inhail	**inhale**		**— innocuous**
inhanse	**enhance**	inordinant	
inherrit	**inherit**		**— inordinate**
inishal	**initial**	inormous	
injary	**injury**		**— enormous**
injeanius		inovate	**innovate**
	— ingenious	inpersonal	
injery	**injury**		**— impersonal**
injoyment		inquier	**inquire**
	— enjoyment	inrich	**enrich**
injustise	**injustice**	insalate	**insulate**
		insalent	**insolent**

73

Incorrect	Correct	Incorrect	Correct
insanaty	**insanity**	instrament	
inscrewtable			**instrument**
	inscrutable	insufrable	
inseck	**insect**		**insufferable**
insendery		intagrate	
	incendiary		**integrate**
insentive		intamate	**intimate**
	incentive	intamediete	
inseprable			**intermediate**
	inseparable	intangle	**entangle**
insest	**incest**	intanjible	
insident	**incident**		**intangible**
insied	**inside**	integeral	**integral**
insinerator		intelectual	
	incinerator		**intellectual**
insipient	**incipient**	intelegance	
insipordinate			**intelligence**
	insubordinate	intemprate	
insise	**incise**		**intemperate**
insistant	**insistent**	intensafy	**intensify**
insite	**insight**	intenshun	
insolluble			**intention**
	insoluble	intercep	**intercept**
insparation		intercorse	
	inspiration		**intercourse**
instagate		interduce	
	instigate		**introduce**
instatute	**institute**	interferance	
insted	**instead**		**interference**
instense	**instance**	interlewd	
instink	**instinct**		**interlude**
instintaneus		intermitent	
	instantaneous		**intermittent**

Incorrect	Correct	Incorrect	Correct
internul —	**internal**	investagate —	
interpalate —			**— investigate**
	— interpolate	invigerate —	
interpet —	**interpret**		**— invigorate**
interrest —	**interest**	invironment —	
intersede —			**— environment**
	— intercede	invit —	**invite**
intersession —		invizable —	
	— intercession		**— invisible**
interupt —		invoise —	**invoice**
	— interrupt	inwerd —	**inward**
intervue —		iradesense —	
	— interview		**— iridescence**
inthusiasm —		irational —	
	— enthusiasm		**— irrational**
intifere —	**interfere**	iredeemable —	
intoragate —			**— irredeemable**
	— interrogate	iregular —	**irregular**
intoxacate —		irelevence —	
	— intoxicate		**— irrelevance**
intracacy —		iresistable —	
	— intricacy		**— irresistible**
intreeg —	**intrigue**	iresistible —	
intresting —			**— irresistible**
	— interesting	iresponsible —	
intrist —	**interest**		**— irresponsible**
inuendo —	**innuendo**	irevocable —	
inurt —	**inert**		**— irrevocable**
invallid —	**invalid**	irigate —	**irrigate**
invazhun —	**invasion**	iritable —	**irritable**
invegel —	**inveigle**	irrascible —	
invenerate —			**— irascible**
	— inveterate		

Incorrect	Correct	Incorrect	Correct
irregardless	— regardless	ishue	— issue
irrelentless	— relentless	ishuence	— issuance
irrevelant	— irrelevant	ismus	— isthmus
isalate	— isolate	itim	— item
isatope	— isotope	ivary	— ivory
isberg	— iceberg	ivey	— ivy
ise	— ice	Izlam	— Islam
Isenhower	— Eisenhower	Izland	— Iceland
		Izrael	— Israel

Look-Alikes or Sound-Alikes

idle (inactive) · idol (false god) · idyll (simple pastoral scene)

I'll (I will) · aisle (passage) · isle (island)

illegible (unreadable) · ineligible (unqualified)

illicit (illegal) · elicit (draw out)

illude (cheat) · allude (refer to)

illusion (false impression) · elusion (evasion, escape by deception) · allusion (reference to)

illusive (deceptive) · allusive (referring to) · elusive (evasive)

imbrue (moisten, especially with blood) · imbue (permeate, color deeply)

imbue (permeate, color deeply) · imbrue (moisten, especially with blood)

immerge (to plunge into) · emerge (to come out)

immersed (plunged in) · emersed (standing out)

immigrant (enters country) · emigrant (leaves country)

imminent (about to happen) · eminent (well-known)

immit (to send in) · emit (to send out)

immoral (evil) · amoral (without a sense of moral responsibility)

immunity (exemption from duty; power to resist disease) · impunity (exemption from punishment or harm)

impassable (closed) · impassible (incapable of being hurt) · impossible (not possible)

impostor (pretender) · imposture (deception)

impunity (exemption from punishment or harm) · immunity (exemption from duty; power to resist disease)

76

in ([prep.] on the inside) · inn (hotel)

inane (pointless) · insane (mad)

incipient (beginning to exist) · insipient (unwise)

incite (stir up) · insight (keen understanding)

indiscreet (unwise) · indiscrete (unseparated)

ineligible (not qualified) · illegible (unreadable)

inequity (injustice) · iniquity (wickedness)

ingenious (original) · ingenuous (innocent)

inn (hotel) · in ([prep.] on the inside)

innervate (to invigorate) · enervate (to deprive of strength)

insane (mad) · inane (pointless)

insert (to put in) · inset (that which is set in)

insight (keen understanding) · incite (stir up)

insipient (unwise) · incipient (beginning to exist)

insulate (to place in a detached situation) · insolate (to expose to the sun)

insurance (protection) · assurance (certainty)

insure (an alternate spelling of ensure) · ensure (to make sure or secure)

intense (in an extreme degree) · intents (purpose)

intern (to act as a hospital intern) · inturn (an inward turn or bend)

internment (state of being detained or held) · interment (burial)

interpellate (to question a minister or executive officer) · interpolate (to alter or insert new matter)

interpolate (to alter or insert new matter) · interpellate (to question a minister or executive officer)

intestate (without a will) · interstate (between states) · intrastate (within state)

inturn (an inward turn or bend) · intern (to act as a hospital intern)

irrelevant (not pertinent) · irreverent (disrespect)

irruption (a bursting in) · eruption (a bursting out)

isle (island) · aisle (passage) · I'll (I will)

it's (it is) · its (belonging to it)

J

Incorrect	Correct	Incorrect	Correct
jackel	jackal	jerney	journey
jacknife	jackknife	jersy	jersey
jael	jail	jeryatricks	geriatrics
jagantic	gigantic	jest	just
jaged	jagged	jetison	jettison
jagwar	jaguar	jety	jetty
jaid	jade	jewellary	jewelry
jakass	jackass	jewls	jewels
jaket	jacket	Jezuit	Jesuit
jale	jail	jieb	jibe
janator	janitor	jiger	jigger
janetic	genetic	jilopy	jalopy
Januwery	January	jimy	jimmy
Jappenese	Japanese	jinjer	ginger
jardineer	jardiniere	jip	gyp
jargin	jargon	jipsee	gypsy
jawndis	jaundice	jiraf	giraffe
jaz	jazz	jirascope	gyroscope
jazmin	jasmine	jiterbug	jitterbug
jeanyal	genial	jober	jobber
Jefersonien	Jeffersonian	jodpurs	jodhpurs
jelatin	gelatine	jokey	jockey
jellus	jealous	jokker	joker
jely	jelly	jokular	jocular
jentile	gentile	joly	jolly
jepordy	jeopardy	jondarm	gendarme

78

Incorrect	Correct	Incorrect	Correct
Jonson (President) — — Johnson		judgement ——— —judgment	
joobilunt — jubilant		judishary — judiciary	
joodishal — judicial		juge ——— judge	
jools ——— jewels		jugler ——— juggler	
joonyer —— junior		jungel ——— jungle	
joorisdicshun ——— — jurisdiction		junkture — juncture	
joose ——— juice		jurie ——— jury	
josle ——— jostle		jurk ——— jerk	
joting ——— jotting		jurnal ——— journal	
joveal ——— jovial		justefy —— justify	
joyus ——— joyous		justise —— justice	
jubalee —— jubilee		juvinile — juvenile	

Look-Alikes or Sound-Alikes

jam (to squeeze; a sweet spread) · **jamb** (side of door)

jealous (envious) · **zealous** (enthusiastic)

jester (clown) · **gesture** (movement)

Jewry (Jews) · **jury** (court)

jibe (to agree; to swing from side to side) · **gibe** (to sneer at)

jinks (lively frolics) · **jinx** (bad luck)

Johnson (President) · **Jonson** (Ben)

joust (to join battle) · **just** (equitable)

juggler (one who juggles) · **jugular** (throat)

just (equitable) · **joust** (to join battle)

K

Incorrect	Correct	Incorrect	Correct
kadet	cadet	kernel	colonel
kaff	calf	kerst	cursed
kahki	khaki	kertin	curtain
kameleon		kerupt	corrupt
	chameleon	kerve	curve
kangeroo		ketch	catch
	kangaroo	ketel	kettle
kanoo	canoe	Khruschev	
kaos	chaos		Khrushchev
kapput	kaput	kiak	kayak
karacter		kibbitzer	kibitzer
	character	kichin	kitchen
karof	carafe	kidnee	kidney
kash	cache	kik	kick
kasm	chasm	kiler	killer
katar	catarrh	killowatt	
kateydid	katydid		kilowatt
kaynine	canine	kimona	kimono
kazm	chasm	kindel	kindle
keal	keel	kindergarden	
kean	keen		kindergarten
kee	key	kindrid	kindred
Keltic	Celtic	kiness	kindness
ken	can	kingdum	
Kenedy	Kennedy		kingdom
kenel	kennel	kiper	kipper
keoty	coyote	kiropedy	
kep	kept		chiropody
kerasene		kist	kissed
	kerosene		

80

Incorrect	Correct	Incorrect	Correct
kitastrofy		koming	coming
	catastrophe	kommunist	
kitin	kitten		communist
kiyoty	coyote	koris	chorus
klak	claque	korz	corps
kleeg	klieg	kraft	craft
kleek	clique	Kremlen	Kremlin
klorine	chlorine	kriptic	cryptic
knifes	knives	kronic	chronic
knoted	knotted	Krushchev	
knowlege			Khrushchev
	knowledge	kugele	cudgel
kolic	colic	kwik	quick
kolyumnist		kwire	choir
	columnist	kwire	quire
komfortable			
	comfortable		

Look-Alikes or Sound-Alikes

kernel (seed) · **colonel** (officer)

key (with lock) · **quay** (dock)

kill (murder) · **kiln** (oven)

knave (fool) · **nave** (part of church)

knead (to press) · **need** (must have)

kneel (to rest on the knees) · **Neal** (man's name)

knew (did know) · **gnu** (animal) · **new** (not old)

knight (feudal rank) · **night** (opposite of day)

knit (form fabric) · **nit** (insect)

knock (to strike) · **nock** (notch of an arrow)

knot (what you tie) · **not** (no)

know (to understand) · **no** (opposite of yes)

knows (understands) · **noes** (negatives) · **nose** (on face)

kohl (eye shadow) · **coal** (fire) · **koel** (a cuckoo)

kola (a nut or tree) · **cola** (a drink)

kris (cheese; dagger) · **crease** (fold)

L

Incorrect	Correct	Incorrect	Correct
labedo	libido	lakwashus	
laber	labor		loquacious
labidinus		lamanate	
	libidinous		laminate
labirinth		lambast	lambaste
	labyrinth	lamentible	
lable	label		lamentable
labratory		lanalin	lanolin
	laboratory	langer	languor
laceing	lacing	langwidge	
lach	latch		language
laciny	larceny	langwish	
lacker	lacquer		languish
lacksitive	laxative	lanlord	landlord
ladel	ladle	lanscape	
lader	ladder		landscape
ladys	ladies	lanse	lance
laffable		lantin	lantern
	laughable	lanzheree	
laffter	laughter		lingerie
lagard	laggard	lapell	lapel
lage	large	larinx	larynx
laging	lagging	lasatude	
laik	lake		lassitude
laim	lame	lase	lace
laison	liaison	laserate	lacerate
lait	late	lasie	lassie
lakey	lackey	lasivious	
lakrimos			lascivious
	lachrymose	laso	lasso

Incorrect	Correct	Incorrect	Correct
latatude —	latitude	leging ——	legging
laticework		legitamate	
	— latticework		— legitimate
latly ——	lately	leif ——	leaf
lattent ——	latent	leige ——	liege
laughible		leisurly —	leisurely
	— laughable	lejable ——	legible
laveleer —	lavaliere	lejend ——	legend
lavinda —	lavender	lejerdeman	
lavitory —	lavatory		— legerdemain
Lawd ——	Lord	lejon ——	legion
lawdible		lekcher —	lecture
	— laudable	lemenade	
lawndry —	laundry		— lemonade
layed ——	laid	lended ——	lent
laywer —	lawyer	lenth ——	length
lazyness —	laziness	lenz ——	lens
leafs ——	leaves	leperd ——	leopard
leakige —	leakage	lepersy —	leprosy
leanyent —	lenient	leprakon	
leasure —	leisure		— leprechaun
leathil ——	lethal	lept ——	leaped
leazon ——	liaison	lern ——	learn
lecksacon —	lexicon	lesen ——	lessen
leconic ——	laconic	less ——	let's
ledgislature		leter ——	letter
	— legislature	lether ——	leather
leeder ——	leader	lethergy —	lethargy
leeg ——	league	letice ——	lettuce
leese ——	lease	letterd ——	lettered
legallize —	legalize	lettup ——	letup
leger ——	ledger	levatation	
legil ——	legal		— levitation

Incorrect	Correct	Incorrect	Correct
leve	leave	limba	limber
leven	eleven	limf	lymph
leven	leaven	limlite	limelight
levle	level	limmit	limit
levler	leveler	Lincon	Lincoln
lew	lieu	Lindon (Johnson) –	
lezbian	lesbian		Lyndon
liberalizm		lingwist	linguist
	liberalism	linier	linear
liberry	library	linkige	linkage
libility	liability	linnen	linen
lible	libel!	linnoleum	
libral	liberal		linoleum
libreto	libretto	linx	lynx
licence	license	liqued	liquid
licker	liquor	liquify	liquefy
lickrish	licorice	liric	lyric
lieing	lying	lisence	license
liem	lime	lisenshus	
lier	liar		licentious
lifboat	lifeboat	lisome	lissome
lifes	lives	lissen	listen
liftime	lifetime	lite	light
ligiment	ligament	litergical	
likeable	likable		liturgical
likker	liquor	litracy	literacy
likly	likely	litrature	
likness	likeness		literature
lillac	lilac	littany	litany
lilly	lily	littul	little
lim	limb	liven	enliven
limazine		livlihood	
	limousine		livelihood

84

Incorrect	Correct	Incorrect	Correct
livly	lively	loover	louver
livry	livery	Loovre	Louvre
lizzard	lizard	looze	lose
lobey	lobby	lor	lore
lobrow	lowbrow	Loraly	Lorelei
locallize	localize	lorel	laurel
locamotive		lornyet	lorgnette
	locomotive	los	loss
lockket	locket	loshun	lotion
lofer	loafer	lotery	lottery
logerithm		lothe	loathe
	logarithm	loveable	lovable
loggic	logic	loveing	loving
loial	loyal	lovly	lovely
loje	lodge	lowd	loud
lokist	locust	lownje	lounge
lokspur	larkspur	lowt	lout
lon	lawn	lubercate	lubricate
lonch	launch	ludacrus	
lonjevaty			ludicrous
	longevity	luet	lute
lonjitude		lugage	luggage
	longitude	luke	luck
lonliness		lukshurient	
	loneliness		luxuriant
lonly	lonely	lukwarm	
lonsome	lonesome		lukewarm
lood	lewd	lulaby	lullaby
loonatic	lunatic	luminecent	
loor	lure		luminescent
loosid	lucid	lunasy	lunacy
lootenant		lunchinet	
	lieutenant		luncheonette

85

Incorrect	Correct	Incorrect	Correct
lushous —	**luscious**	luxry ——	**luxury**
lusterous —	**lustrous**	lyeing ——	**lying**
luv ——	**love**	lyon ——	**lion**

Look-Alikes or Sound-Alikes

lain (did lie on) · lane (path)

lair (den) · layer (a thickness; fold)

lam (run away) · lamb (young sheep)

laser (a beam of coherent light) · lazar (a leper)

later (afterwards) · latter (the last one of two)

lath (strip of wood) · lathe (a machine tool)

laud (praise) · lord (a noble)

lay (to deposit) · lei (a wreath)

lazar (a leper) · laser (a beam of coherent light)

lead (metal; to guide) · led (did guide)

leaf (tree) · lief (gladly)

leak (crack) · leek (vegetable)

lean (thin) · lien (legal charge)

least (smallest) · lest (unless)

lessee (tenant) · lesser (smaller) · lessor (one who leases)

lessen (to decrease) · lesson (instruction)

levee (dike) · levy (fine, tax)

liable (obligated) · libel (slander)

liar (tells lies) · lyre (musical instrument)

licorice (a flavoring) · lickerish (eager, craving)

lie (falsehood) · lye (chemical)

lief (gladly) · leaf (tree)

lien (legal charge) · lean (thin)

lightening (making lighter, relieving) · lightning (flash in sky)

linage (number of lines) · lineage (ancestry)

lineament (one of the contours of the body) · liniment (a thin ointment)

links (joins) · lynx (animal)

liqueur (sweet liquor) · liquor (alcoholic drink)

lo! (exclamation) · low (down; base)

load (burden) · lode (mineral)

loan (lending) · lone (alone)

loath (reluctant) · loathe (despise)

local (not widespread) · locale (a locality)

loch (lake) · lock (fastening)

locks (fastenings) · lox (salmon)

locus (a place; locality) · locust (insect)

loose (not tight) · lose (fail to win)

86

loot (booty) · **lute** (musical instrument)
lord (noble) · **laud** (praise)
lumbar (part of body) · **lumber** (wood)

luxuriance (state of being luxurious) · **luxuriant** (exceedingly fertile) · **luxurious** (sumptuous)
lye (chemical) · **lie** (falsehood)
lynx (animal) · **links** (joins)

M

Incorrect	Correct	Incorrect	Correct
macarune		maibe	**maybe**
	macaroon	maidnly	
maccadim			**maidenly**
	macadam	mainger	**manger**
maccaroni		mainia	**mania**
	macaroni	maintainance	
machurashun			**maintenance**
	maturation	maionaize	
machure	**mature**		**mayonnaise**
macintosh		maitriarc	
	mackintosh		**matriarch**
mackrel	**mackerel**	majer	**major**
madalion		majik	**magic**
	medallion	majistrat	
maddame			**magistrate**
	madame	majoraty	
madmwazel			**majority**
	mademoiselle	Makavelian	
madres	**madras**		**Machiavellian**
magizine		makeing	**making**
	magazine	maladikshun	
magnatude			**malediction**
	magnitude	malase	**malice**
magnifasense		malfezence	
	magnificence		**malfeasance**
magnit	**magnet**	maliable	
magot	**maggot**		**malleable**
magnut	**magnet**	maline	**malign**
mahiraja		malingger	
	maharajah		**malinger**

88

Incorrect	Correct	Incorrect	Correct
malishus		manuscrip	
	— malicious		— manuscript
mallady	— malady	manur	— manner
mallis	— malice	manuver	
mamal	— mammal		— maneuver
mamalade		mapul	— maple
	— marmalade	maraskino	
mamuth			— maraschino
	— mammoth	maratime	
manacure			— maritime
	— manicure	marawana	
manafacture			— marijuana
	— manufacture	marbel	— marble
manafesto		mareen	— marine
	— manifesto	marige	— marriage
manafold		marjerin	
	— manifold		— margarine
managable		marjin	— margin
	— manageable	markee	— marquis
manajer	— manager	markez	
manditory			— marquise
	— mandatory	markit	— market
maner	— manner	marod	— maraud
manicle	— manacle	marow	— marrow
manje	— mange	marriagable	
manjer	— manger		— marriageable
manogamist		marrie	— marry
	— monogamist	marryed	— married
manotinus		marteeni	— martini
	— monotonous	marter	— martyr
manshun	— mansion	marune	— maroon
mantlpeace		marvilus	
	— mantelpiece		— marvelous

Incorrect	Correct	Incorrect	Correct
masaje —	**massage**	maxamum —	
masaker —	**massacre**		**— maximum**
mascuelin —		maylanje —	**mélange**
	— masculine	mazoleum —	
mashety —	**machete**		**— mausoleum**
mashinery —		meaness —	
	— machinery		**— meanness**
Masichusetts —		meanyal —	**menial**
	— Massachusetts	mecanic —	
masinry —	**masonry**		**— mechanic**
masive —	**massive**	Medacare —	
maskerade —			**— Medicare**
	— masquerade	medamorfisis —	
masta —	**master**		**— metamorphosis**
mastacate —		medecine —	
	— masticate		**— medicine**
masur —	**masseur**	medeocker —	
mater —	**matter**		**— mediocre**
mater de —		Mediteranean —	
	— maître d'		**— Mediterranean**
maternaty —		medl —	**medal**
	— maternity	medle —	**meddle**
mathamatics —		medly —	**medley**
	— mathematics	medow —	**meadow**
matinay —	**matinée**	meedjum —	
matramony —			**— medium**
	— matrimony	meeger —	**meager**
matrinly —	**matronly**	meeteor —	**meteor**
matris —	**mattress**	meglomania —	
matterial —			**— megalomania**
	— material	mein —	**mien**
mavrick —		mekanize —	
	— maverick		**— mechanize**

90

Incorrect	Correct	Incorrect	Correct
melincoly		mercinery	
	— melancholy		— mercenary
mellodrama		merderer	
	— melodrama		— murderer
mellodious		merdger — merger	
	— melodious	meret — merit	
mellon —— melon		merly — merely	
melow — mellow		mermer	
memberane			— murmur
	— membrane	merryly — merrily	
memmento		mersy — mercy	
	— memento	mesenger	
memmorial			— messenger
	— memorial	mesure — measure	
memrable		mesy — messy	
	— memorable	mesyur — monsieur	
memry — memory		metafor	
memwar — memoir			— metaphor
menajery		meterial — material	
	— menagerie	Methadist	
menise — menace			— Methodist
menshun		metripolitan	
	— mention		— metropolitan
ment —— meant		mettalic — metallic	
menstrate		metul — metal	
	— menstruate	meucus — mucous	
mentle — mental		mezaneen	
meny —— many			— mezzanine
menyu — menu		mezels — measles	
merang		mezmerize	
	— meringue		— mesmerize
merchindize		micrascope	
	— merchandise		— microscope

Incorrect	Correct	Incorrect	Correct
miday	midday	miopia	myopia
middel	middle	miricle	miracle
midevil	medieval	miror	mirror
mikature	mixture	mirraje	mirage
milage	mileage	mirtle	myrtle
milatery	military	mischevous	
milenium			mischievous
	millennium	mischif	mischief
milinary		mise	mice
	millinery	miselaneous	
milionaire			miscellaneous
	millionaire	mishin	mission
millicha	militia	Misissippi	
minamum			Mississippi
	minimum	mislayed	mislaid
Minasota		mispell	misspell
	Minnesota	misquito	mosquito
minature		misrable	
	miniature		miserable
mingel	mingle	misry	misery
miniral	mineral	missconduct	
minis	minus		misconduct
miniscule		missel	missile
	minuscule	misselaneous	
ministor	minister		miscellaneous
minit	minute	missfortune	
minnimum			misfortune
	minimum	misshap	mishap
minoraty		missojiny	
	minority		misogyny
minse	mince	misstake	mistake
minusha		mistacizm	
	minutiae		mysticism

92

Incorrect	Correct	Incorrect	Correct
mistate	misstate	mollestation	— molestation
misterious	— mysterious	mombo	mambo
mistery	mystery	mommentus	— momentous
mistify	mystify	monark	monarch
mistris	mistress	mone	moan
mithical	mythical	monistery	— monastery
mittin	mitten	monitone	— monotone
mizer	miser	monopolly	— monopoly
mizerable	— miserable	monsterous	— monstrous
moap	mope	mony	money
mobillize	— mobilize	moraleity	— morality
mocassin	— moccasin	moray	moiré
modifyer	modifier	Moreman	— Mormon
modil	model	morfeen	— morphine
modist	modest	morg	morgue
modlin	maudlin	morgage	— mortgage
modren	modern	mornfull	— mournful
Mohamedin	— Muhammadan	moroco	morocco
mohoginy	— mahogany	morsal	morsel
mojulate	— modulate	mortafy	mortify
mokery	mockery	mortaly	mortally
molatto	mulatto		
molify	mollify		
mollecule	— molecule		

93

Incorrect	Correct	Incorrect	Correct
mortuery	— **mortuary**	multaply	— **multiply**
moshin	**motion**	mundain	— **mundane**
mosk	**mosque**	munkey	**monkey**
mosy	**mossy**	munth	**month**
mote	**moat**	murmer	**murmur**
moteef	**motif**	musell	**muscle**
moter	**motor**	musilije	**mucilage**
motled	**mottled**	mustid	**mustard**
moustache	— **mustache**	mutny	**mutiny**
movment	— **movement**	muzeem	**museum**
moyschur	**moisture**	muzik	**music**
mozaic	**mosaic**	muzlin	**muslin**
mudy	**muddy**	myazma	**miasma**
muleish	**mulish**	mygrate	**migrate**

Look-Alikes or Sound-Alikes

made (did make) · maid (servant)

magna (great) · magma (rock)

magnate (prominent person) · magnet (attract iron)

mail (letters) · male (man)

main (principal) · mane (hair of animal)

maize (corn) · maze (confusing paths)

manner (method) · manor (estate)

mantel (shelf at fireplace) · mantle (cloak)

marc (refuse remaining after pressing seeds, fruits) · mark (sign)

marital (in marriage) · martial (warlike) · Marshall (the General or the Plan)

marshal (official) · martial (warlike) · Marshall (the General or the Plan)

mark (sign) · marc (refuse remaining after pressing seeds, fruits)

marriage (wedding) · mirage (illusion)

marry (wed) · merry (gay) · Mary (girl's name)

mascle (a steel plate) · muscle (an organ of the body) · mussel (shellfish)

mason (brick layer) · meson (in physics, a particle)

94

massed (assembled) · mast (on boat)

mast (on boat) · massed (assembled)

maybe (perhaps) · may be (may happen)

maze (confusing paths) · maize (corn)

mean (nasty) · mien (bearing)

meat (food) · meet (encounter)

medal (award) · meddle (interfere) · mettle (spirit) · metal (material)

merry (gay) · Mary (girl's name) · marry (wed)

meson (in physics, a particle) · mason (brick layer)

meteorology (study of atmosphere) · metrology (system of weights and measures)

mews (cat's sound; row of stables) · muse (think)

might (strength; may) · mite (small insect; small child)

mil (unit of measure) · mill (grinding machine; factory)

millenary (a thousand) · millinery (hats)

millinery (hats) · millenary (a thousand)

mince (to cut into small pieces) · mints (places where money is made; candies)

mind (brain) · mined (dug)

miner (one who mines) · minor (below legal age; unimportant)

mints (places where money is made) · mince (to cut into small pieces)

mirage (illusion) · marriage (wedding)

Miss (single woman) · Mrs. (married woman) · mss. (manuscripts)

missal (book for Mass) · missile (weapon)

missed (failed) · mist (haze)

moat (ditch) · mote (small particle)

mode (manner) · mowed (cut down)

moral (lesson) · morale (spirit)

morn (morning) · mourn (grieve)

morning (A.M.) · mourning (grieving)

mote (small particle) · moat (ditch)

motif (theme) · motive (reason)

mudder (a horse) · mother (a female parent)

muscle (of body) · mussel (shellfish) · mascle (a steel plate)

muse (think) · mews (cat's sound; row of stables)

Muslim (religion) · muslin (cloth)

mustard (spice) · mustered (summoned)

N

Incorrect	Correct	Incorrect	Correct
nabor	**neighbor**	nat	**gnat**
nachurally		natchur	**nature**
	naturally	Natzi	**Nazi**
nack	**knack**	nausha	**nausea**
nacotics	**narcotics**	navagible	
nafairius			**navigable**
	nefarious	navey	**navy**
naftha	**naphtha**	naw	**gnaw**
naged	**nagged**	naybor	**neighbor**
Nahru	**Nehru**	nazal	**nasal**
naivtay	**naïveté**	nebulus	**nebulous**
nale	**nail**	necesery	
namless	**nameless**		**necessary**
namonia		necesity	
	pneumonia		**necessity**
napsack	**knapsack**	neckromansy	
naration			**necromancy**
	narration	nectereen	
narative	**narrative**		**nectarine**
narl	**gnarl**	nee	**knee**
narow	**narrow**	needel	**needle**
narsistic		neet	**neat**
	narcissistic	neether	**neither**
nasent	**nascent**	nefew	**nephew**
nash	**gnash**	negitive	**negative**
nashunel	**national**	neglajence	
nastershum			**negligence**
	nasturtium	negleck	**neglect**
nastyness		neglegay	
	nastiness		**negligee**

Incorrect	Correct	Incorrect	Correct
negoshiate		nicknack	
	— negotiate		— knickknack
Negros	— **Negroes**	Nickson	— **Nixon**
neice	**niece**	nicly	**nicely**
nek	**neck**	nieve	**naïve**
nekachif		nife	**knife**
	— neckerchief	nill	**nil**
nekkid	— **naked**	nimbel	— **nimble**
neks	**next**	nimf	— **nymph**
nemonic		ninedy	— **ninety**
	— mnemonic	nineth	— **ninth**
neppotizm		ninteen	— **nineteen**
	— nepotism	ninty	— **ninety**
nere	**near**	nippal	— **nipple**
nerse	**nurse**	nite	**night**
nerviss	— **nervous**	nob	— **knob**
nesecery		nobles oblege	
	— necessary		— noblesse oblige
nesessity		noblman	
	—necessity		— nobleman
nesle	**nestle**	nocean	— **notion**
neumatic		noch	— **notch**
	— pneumatic	nock	— **knock**
neumonia		nockternil	
	— pneumonia		— nocturnal
newsance		noisesome	— **noisome**
	— nuisance	nokshus	— **noxious**
Niagra	— **Niagara**	noll	— **knoll**
nializm	— **nihilism**	nome	— **gnome**
nible	**nibble**	nomminate	
nicateen	— **nicotine**		— nominate
nich	**niche**	nonnentity	
nickle	**nickel**		— nonentity

97

Incorrect	Correct	Incorrect	Correct
nonshalant		nucleous — **nucleus**	
	— **nonchalant**	nudaty — **nudity**	
noo	**new**	nuklear — **nuclear**	
nooclear — **nuclear**		nulification	
nooratic — **neurotic**			— **nullification**
noosance		num	**numb**
	— **nuisance**	numbskull	
noot	**knout**		— **numskull**
nootral — **neutral**		numrous	
noovo reesh			— **numerous**
	— **nouveau riche**	nunery — **nunnery**	
normel — **normal**		nupshal — **nuptial**	
northernly		nuralja — **neuralgia**	
	— **northerly**	nurish — **nourish**	
notery — **notary**		nuritis — **neuritis**	
noth	**north**	nuroligist	
notible — **notable**			— **neurologist**
noticable		nurserys	
	— **noticeable**		— **nurseries**
notise	**notice**	nursmaid	
nottorious			— **nursemaid**
	— **notorious**	nusence — **nuisance**	
noval	**novel**	nustaljic — **nostalgic**	
novis	**novice**	nuthing — **nothing**	
no where		nutralise	
	— **nowhere**		— **neutralize**
nowlege		nutrishon	
	— **knowledge**		— **nutrition**
noyz	**noise**	nutting — **nothing**	
nozgay — **nosegay**		nuty — **nutty**	
nu	**new**	nyeev — **naïve**	
nuckle — **knuckle**		nyether — **neither**	
		nyew	**new**

Look-Alikes or Sound-Alikes

NASA (space agency) · Nasser (President of Egypt)

naval (navy) · navel (stomach)

nave (part of church) · knave (fool)

nay (no) · neigh (horse's sound)

Neal (man's name) · kneel (to rest on the knees)

need (lack) · knead (to press)

new (not old) · knew (did know) · gnu (animal)

night (opposite of day) · knight (feudal rank)

nit (insect) · knit (form fabric)

no (opposite of yes) · know (to understand)

noble (aristocratic) · Nobel (the prize)

nocturn (a midnight prayer) · nocturne (musical composition)

noes (negatives) · nose (on face) · knows (understands)

none (not one) · nun (religious)

not (no) · knot (what you tie)

O

Incorrect	Correct	Incorrect	Correct
obay	obey	obvius	obvious
obcelete	obsolete	obzervance	observance
obedeance	obedience	ocasion	occasion
obees	obese	occassionel	occasional
obichuary	obituary	occer	occur
obitrator	arbitrator	occulist	oculist
objeck	object	occupent	occupant
objecshunable	objectionable	occupyed	occupied
obleck	oblique	occurance	occurrence
oblidge	oblige	octapus	octopus
obligatto	obbligato	ocupancy	occupancy
obnocshus	obnoxious	ocurr	occur
obseekweus	obsequious	od	odd
obseen	obscene	Oddisy	Odyssey
obseshun	obsession	oder	odor
obsolecent	obsolescent	oderus	odorous
obstatrishin	obstetrician	ofen	often
obstickal	obstacle	ofer	offer
obstonite	obstinate	offence	offense
		offring	offering
		ofice	office
		oficial	official
		ofishus	officious
		ofthamology	ophthalmology

P

Incorrect	Correct	Incorrect	Correct
pachezi	— parcheesi	pandcake	— pancake
packige	package	panerama	— panorama
Packistan	— Pakistan	panicea	panacea
padestrian	— pedestrian	panicy	panicky
padjama	pajama	panitela	— panatella
padray	padre	pannel	panel
pagent	pageant	pantamine	— pantomime
pakage	package	panyless	— penniless
pakt	pact	panzy	pansy
pallace	palace	paper-mashe	— papier-mâché
pallacial	palatial	papisy	papacy
pallasade	— palisade	pappriker	paprika
pallatable	— palatable	parafrase	— paraphrase
pallit	palate	paralise	paralyze
pallsey	palsy	pardner	partner
palpatate	— palpitate	parfay	parfait
palpible	palpable	paridice	paradise
pam	palm	parifernalia	— paraphernalia
pamistry	— palmistry	parisite	parasite
pamphalet	— pamphlet	parkay	parquet
pandamoneum	— pandemonium	parlement	— parliament

Incorrect	Correct	Incorrect	Correct
oger	ogre	ontray	entrée
ogil	ogle	onvelope	— envelope
oister	oyster	Oo Thant	— U Thant
ole	old	opaik	opaque
olfaktry	olfactory	openess	openness
Olimpic	Olympic	opin	open
ollive	olive	opinyun	opinion
omishin	omission	opis	opus
omisible	omissible	oponent	— opponent
omlet	omelet	oportune	— opportune
omminous	— ominous	oportunity	— opportunity
ommitt	omit	opose	oppose
omnishent	— omniscient	opperator	— operator
omniverus	— omnivorous	oppeum	opium
onarus	onerous	opponant	— opponent
oncore	encore	opra	opera
onest	honest	oprate	operate
on mass	en masse	opresser	— oppressor
onor	honor	opreta	operetta
onorable	— honorable	opry	opera
onorary	honorary	opshinul	optional
onroot	en route	optishin	optician
onsomble	— ensemble	optomism	— optimism
ontoroge	— entourage	oragin	origin
ontraprenor	— entrepreneur		

Incorrect	Correct	Incorrect	Correct
orbut	orbit	oscullatory	
orchester			osculatory
	orchestra	oshan	ocean
ordinence		osheanografi	
	ordinance		oceanography
ordinry	ordinary	osify	ossify
ore	oar	osillate	oscillate
orevoir	au revoir	osstensible	
orfan	orphan		ostensible
orful	awful	ostintashus	
organisation			ostentatious
	organization	othe	oath
orgazm	orgasm	our's	ours
orgin	organ	ourselfs	
oricul	oracle		ourselves
orignal	original	outragous	
oringe	orange		outrageous
orjy	orgy	outsidder	
orkid	orchid		outsider
orniment		outter	outer
	ornament	outwerd	outward
orrator	orator	ovature	overture
ors d'oeurves		overate	overrate
	hors d'oeuvres	overeach	
orstritch	ostrich		overreach
orthentik		overought	
	authentic		overwrought
ortherdox		overser	overseer
	orthodox	overun	overrun
orthorety		overwelm	
	authority		overwhelm
orthorize		overy	ovary
	authorize	ovurt	overt

Incorrect	Correct	Incorrect	Cor
ownce	ounce	oyl	
owst	oust	oyntment	
oxagen	oxygen		ointm
oxes	oxen		

Look-Alikes or Sound-Alikes

oar (boat) · o'er (over) · or (alternative) · ore (mineral) · awe (fear)

ode (poem) · owed (did owe)

of (belonging to) · off (away from)

older (refers to age only) · elder (refers to age and wisdom gained)

one (single) · won (did win)

opposite (other side) · apposite (suitable)

oral (verbal) · aural (hearic

ordinance (law) · ordnanc (military supply)

oscillate (vibrate) · oscula (kiss)

ought (should) · aught (zer

our (belongs to us) · hour (time)

owed (did owe) · ode (poe

102

103

Incorrect	Correct	Incorrect	Correct
parler	**parlor**	parrymecium	
Parmizan cheese			**paramecium**
	Parmesan	parry-mutual	
parodocks			**pari-mutuel**
	paradox	parsel	**parcel**
parot	**parrot**	parshel	**partial**
parraboler		partasiple	
	parabola		**participle**
parrade	**parade**	partative	
parrafin	**paraffin**		**partitive**
parragraf		partickle	**particle**
	paragraph	partickuler	
parralel	**parallel**		**particular**
parralisis		partishun	
	paralysis		**partition**
parramount		partisipate	
	paramount		**participate**
parratrooper		partizan	**partisan**
	paratrooper	partys	**parties**
parrenthasis		parynoia	
	parenthesis		**paranoia**
parrible	**parable**	parypledgic	
parridy	**parody**		**paraplegic**
parrikeet		pasay	**passé**
	parakeet	pashent	**patient**
parrish	**parish**	pashion	**passion**
parrishute		pasible	**passable**
	parachute	pasidge	**passage**
parrity	**parity**	Pasific	**Pacific**
parrocheal		pasify	**pacify**
	parochial	pasive	**passive**
parrole	**parole**	paso	**peso**
parrson	**parson**		

Incorrect	Correct	Incorrect	Correct
pasport —	**passport**	paveing ——	**paving**
passifist —	**pacifist**	pavilon —	**pavilion**
passta ———	**pasta**	pavment ———	
passtell ——	**pastel**		**— pavement**
passtime ———		pawlbarer ———	
	— pastime		**— pallbearer**
passtrami ———		payed ———	**paid**
	— pastrami	paysley —	**paisley**
pastachio ———		payso ———	**peso**
	— pistachio	paythos —	**pathos**
pasteing —	**pasting**	pean —	**paean**
paster ———	**pastor**	peavish —	**peevish**
pastrey —	**pastry**	pecunerary ———	
pasturize ———			**— pecuniary**
	— pasteurize	pedagree ———	
patata ———	**potato**		**— pedigree**
patern —	**pattern**	pedistal —	**pedestal**
paticular ———		peeanist —	**pianist**
	— particular	peech ———	**peach**
patition —	**petition**	peedyatrics ———	
patritism ———			**— pediatrics**
	— patriotism	peenil ———	**penal**
patriyot ——	**patriot**	peenut ———	**peanut**
patroleum ———		peepul —	**people**
	— petroleum	peeza ———	**pizza**
pattedifoigra ———		pegoda —	**pagoda**
— pâté de foie gras		peice ——	**piece**
pattent ——	**patent**	peirce ——	**pierce**
patternal ———		pekan ——	**pecan**
	— paternal	pelet ———	**pellet**
pattio ———	**patio**	pellmell —	**pall-mall**
patren ——	**patron**	pemanship ———	
pattrol ——	**patrol**		**— penmanship**

Incorrect	Correct	Incorrect	Correct
penant	**pennant**	perculiar	**peculiar**
penatenshary	**penitentiary**	percushion	**percussion**
penatint	**penitent**	perdict	**predict**
penatrate	**penetrate**	perdikament	**predicament**
penelty	**penalty**	perdominant	**predominant**
penife	**penknife**	perel	**peril**
penndyalum	**pendulum**	perfer	**prefer**
pennicilan	**penicillin**	perferate	**perforate**
penninsuler	**peninsula**	perfessor	**professor**
penntegon	**pentagon**	perfict	**perfect**
penoir	**peignoir**	perge	**purge**
pensil	**pencil**	perliminary	**preliminary**
Pensylvania	**Pennsylvania**	permenant	**permanent**
Pentacostal	**Pentecostal**	permiate	**permeate**
peraps	**perhaps**	permisable	**permissible**
percalator	**percolator**	permitt	**permit**
percarious	**precarious**	permonition	**premonition**
percaution	**precaution**	perpare	**prepare**
percept	**precept**	perpatrate	**perpetrate**
percieve	**perceive**	perpettual	**perpetual**
percise	**precise**		
perclude	**preclude**		

107

Incorrect	Correct	Incorrect	Correct
perpindicular ——		perser —— purser	
	— **perpendicular**	perserve — **preserve**	
perple —— **purple**		persikute ——	
perponderant ——			— **persecute**
	— **preponderant**	persin —— **person**	
perport — **purport**		persistance ——	
perposterous ——			— **persistence**
	— **preposterous**	personnal ——	
perpulsion ——			— **personal**
	— **propulsion**	perspacacous ——	
perranum ——			— **perspicacious**
	— **per annum**	persue — **pursue**	
perrascope ——		persuit — **pursuit**	
	— **periscope**	persumption ——	
perrenial ——			— **presumption**
	— **perennial**	perswade ——	
perrifery ——			— **persuade**
	— **periphery**	pertanint ——	
perrimter ——			— **pertinent**
	— **perimeter**	pertato — **potato**	
perriod — **period**		pertend — **pretend**	
perrish —— **perish**		perticulars ——	
perroxide — **peroxide**			— **particulars**
persavere ——		pertition — **petition**	
	— **persevere**	pervail — **prevail**	
perscribe ——		pervention ——	
	— **prescribe**		— **prevention**
perscription ——		pervide — **provide**	
	— **prescription**	pesimist — **pessimist**	
perse —— **purse**		pestaside ——	
persent — **percent**			— **pesticide**
persepectus ——		petteet —— **petite**	
	— **prospectus**	pettle —— **petal**	

Incorrect	Correct	Incorrect	Correct
pettrify	petrify	phisyotherapy —	
pettulant			— physiotherapy
	— petulant	phonettic	
pettycoat			— phonetic
	— petticoat	phonnics —	phonics
peverse —	perverse	phosferous	
pezint —	peasant		— phosphorus
Pharow —	Pharaoh	phosforresence	
phasician			— phosphorescence
	— physician	photagraph	
phaze —	phase		— photograph
Pheenix —	Phoenix	phylanthropy	
pheenobarbatal —			— philanthropy
	— phenobarbital	physiclly	
Philipino			— physically
	— Filipino	piana —	piano
Philis —	Phyllis	piaza —	piazza
phillately		picadilo	
	— philately		— peccadillo
Phillidelphia		piccyune	
	— Philadelphia		— picayune
Phillipines		pich —	pitch
	— Philippines	pickel —	pickle
phinomenon		picknic —	picnic
	— phenomenon	picollo —	piccolo
phisics —	physics	pidgeon —	pigeon
phisionomy		pietty —	piety
	— physiognomy	piggment	
phisique			— pigment
	— physique	pika —	pica
phisyology		piket —	picket
	— physiology	pilage —	pillage
		pilbox —	pillbox

Incorrect	Correct	Incorrect	Correct
pileing	piling	pittuitary	pituitary
pilet	pilot	pitty	pity
pilgrum	pilgrim	pityful	pitiful
piller	pillar	pivit	pivot
pillery	pilory	placcate	placate
pillfer	pilfer	plackard	placard
pillgrim	pilgrim	placment	placement
pimmento	pimento	plad	plaid
pimpel	pimple	plage	plague
pinacle	pinnacle	plajiarism	plagiarism
pinapple	pineapple	plannet	planet
pinnochle	pinochle	plannetarium	planetarium
pinnup	pinup	plasa	plaza
pinsers	pincers	plasebo	placebo
pinurious	penurious	plassid	placid
pionner	pioneer	plasstic	plastic
pipeing	piping	platow	plateau
piramid	pyramid	plater	platter
pire	pyre	plattform	platform
pirex	Pyrex	plattinum	platinum
piromaniac	pyromaniac	plattitude	platitude
pirotechnics	pyrotechnics	plattonic	platonic
pistin	piston	plattoon	platoon
pitchur	picture	plausable	plausible
pitence	pittance		
pittfall	pitfall		
Pittsburg	Pittsburgh		

110

Incorrect	Correct	Incorrect	Correct
plazma	**plasma**	poit	**poet**
plebbacite		poize	**poise**
	plebiscite	poka	**polka**
plee	**plea**	polen	**pollen**
pleed	**plead**	poler	**polar**
pleet	**pleat**	polerise	**polarize**
pleeze	**please**	poletry	**poultry**
plege	**pledge**	polisy	**policy**
plenery	**plenary**	Pollaris	**Polaris**
plentyful		Pollaroid	
	plentiful		**Polaroid**
plesant	**pleasant**	pollemic	**polemic**
plesure	**pleasure**	pollice	**police**
plethorra		polligamy	
	plethora		**polygamy**
plite	**plight**	pollio	**polio**
pluerisy	**pleurisy**	pollish	**polish**
plumer	**plumber**	pollite	**polite**
plurel	**plural**	pollitics	**politics**
pluss	**plus**	pollyethelene	
pluttonium			**polyethylene**
	plutonium	pollygon	**polygon**
plyable	**pliable**	polute	**pollute**
plyers	**pliers**	pome	**poem**
pocession		pommade	
	possession		**pomade**
pockabook		pompidor	
	pocketbook		**pompadour**
pockit	**pocket**	pompus	
poggrom	**pogrom**		**pompous**
poinyant		Pontif	**Pontiff**
	poignant	pooding	**pudding**
poisin	**poison**	poppular	**popular**

111

Incorrect	Correct	Incorrect	Correct
porcelin — **porcelain**		povety — **poverty**	
poridge — **porridge**		powt — **pout**	
pornagraphy — **pornography**		poynsetta — **poinsettia**	
porposal — **proposal**		praier — **prayer**	
portfollio — **portfolio**		prairy — **prairie**	
portible — **portable**		praize — **praise**	
portrit — **portrait**		praktical — **practical**	
posative — **positive**		praktise — **practice**	
posess — **possess**		preceed — **precede**	
posession — **possession**		preceive — **perceive**	
posible — **possible**		precink — **precinct**	
pospone — **postpone**		precoshious — **precocious**	
possable — **possible**		precure — **procure**	
possition — **position**		predacate — **predicate**	
possy — **posse**		preddesessor — **predecessor**	
postel — **postal**		predick — **predict**	
postige — **postage**		predictible — **predictable**	
postyure — **posture**		predjudice — **prejudice**	
potenshal — **potential**		preeamble — **preamble**	
potery — **pottery**		preech — **preach**	
pottasium — **potassium**		preefabrikate — **prefabricate**	
poturri — **potpourri**		preffer — **prefer**	
pouder — **powder**		prefice — **preface**	
pounse — **pounce**		prefrence — **preference**	

Incorrect	Correct	Incorrect	Correct
pregenitor —		presadent —	
	— **progenitor**		— **president**
pregnent —		Presbaterian —	
	— **pregnant**		— **Presbyterian**
preist —	**priest**	presedent —	
prelliminary —			— **precedent**
	— **preliminary**	preseed — **precede**	
prelood — **prelude**		presept — **precept**	
preminent —		preshure — **pressure**	
	— **pr eeminent**	preshus — **precious**	
premire — **premier**		presice — **precise**	
premiss — **premise**		presipatate —	
premiture —			— **precipitate**
	— **premature**	prespiration —	
premival —			— **perspiration**
	— **primeval**	prespire — **perspire**	
premmonition —		president —	
	— **premonition**		— **president**
premyum —		presstige — **prestige**	
	— **premium**	prestege — **prestige**	
preocupation —		prety — **pretty**	
	— **preoccupation**	prevade — **pervade**	
preperation —		prevale — **prevail**	
	— **preparation**	prevelant —	
prepetual —			— **prevalent**
	— **perpetual**	previus — **previous**	
preposal —		prevlent — **prevalent**	
	— **proposal**	prevue — **preview**	
preppare — **prepare**		preycis — **precis**	
prepposition —		prezent — **present**	
	— **preposition**	prezide — **preside**	
preprietor —		prezident —	
	— **proprietor**		— **president**

Incorrect	Correct	Incorrect	Correct
prezume	— presume	proddigious	— prodigious
prickley	prickly	proddigy	prodigy
pricless	priceless	produck	product
prie	pry	produse	produce
primative	— primitive	profecy	— prophecy
primery	primary	profer	proffer
prinsess	princess	profeshun	— profession
priorty	priority	proffesor	— professor
pritify	prettify	proffess	profess
prity	pretty	profficient	— proficient
privaricate	— prevaricate	proffile	profile
priviledge	— privilege	proffit	profit
privisy	privacy	proflagate	— profligate
privite	private	profuce	profuse
prizm	prism	profunctory	— perfunctory
prizon	prison	proggnosis	— prognosis
probible	— probable	proggres	progress
problim	problem	programm	— program
proccreate	— procreate	prohibbit	prohibit
procede	proceed	projeck	project
proceedure	— procedure	projeny	progeny
procent	percent	prokrastinate	— procrastinate
proclame	— proclaim		
procter	proctor		

114

Incorrect	Correct	Incorrect	Correct
prollific	— **prolific**	propposition	— **proposition**
prologgue	— **prologue**	propprietor	— **proprietor**
prominade	— **promenade**	proppulsion	— **propulsion**
promisary	— **promissory**	proprity	— **propriety**
prommenade	— **promenade**	prosedure	— **procedure**
prommice	— **promise**	prosess	— **process**
prommiscuous	— **promiscuous**	prossecute	— **prosecute**
prommote	— **promote**	prossession	— **procession**
promt	— **prompt**	prosspect	— **prospect**
pronounciation	— **pronunciation**	prosstate	— **prostate**
prood	— **prude**	prosstatute	— **prostitute**
proove	— **prove**	protatype	— **prototype**
properganda	— **propaganda**	proteck	— **protect**
proppagate	— **propagate**	protene	— **protein**
proppel	— **propel**	protude	— **protrude**
propper	— **proper**	prottaganist	— **protagonist**
propperty	— **property**	prottaplasm	— **protoplasm**
propponent	— **proponent**	prottegay	— **protégé**
propportion	— **proportion**	prottest	— **protest**
proppose	— **propose**	Prottestent	— **Protestant**

Incorrect	Correct	Incorrect	Correct
prottocoll	——	punative —	**punitive**
	— protocol	punctull —	**punctual**
protton ——	**proton**	pungture	——
provadents	——		**— puncture**
	— providence	punjint ——	**pungent**
provoak —	**provoke**	punktuate	——
prowd ——	**proud**		**— punctuate**
proxximmity	——	punnish —	**punish**
	— proximity	pupet ——	**puppet**
proxxy ——	**proxy**	pupull ——	**pupil**
prozaic —	**prosaic**	purchise	——
psam ——	**psalm**		**— purchase**
psycology	——	purgery —	**perjury**
	— psychology	purile ——	**puerile**
psyconalasis		purjery —	**perjury**
	— psychoanalysis	purpise —	**purpose**
publick ——	**public**	pursavere	
puding —	**pudding**		**— persevere**
pudjy ——	**pudgy**	pursuade	——
pue ——————	**pew**		**— persuade**
pujjy ——	**pudgy**	purterb —	**perturb**
pulit ——	**pullet**	Purto Rico	
pulkritude	——		**— Puerto Rico**
	— pulchritude	pussilanamous	——
pullminary	——		**— pusillanimous**
	— pulmonary	putred —	**putrid**
pullpit ——	**pulpit**	putrify —	**putrefy**
pullverise		puzzel —	**puzzle**
	— pulverize	pweblo —	**pueblo**
pumkin	——	pyaneer —	**pioneer**
	— pumpkin	Pyric victory	——
pumpanickle	——		**— Pyrrhic victory**
	— pumpernickel	pyus ——	**pious**

Look-Alikes or Sound-Alikes

packed (bundled) · pact (agreement)

paean (hymn of joy) · peon (peasant)

pail (bucket) · pale (enclosure; lacking color)

pain (ache) · pane (window)

pair (two) · pare (shave) · pear (fruit)

palate (taste) · palette (artist's board) · pallet (platform)

pall (covering; gloomy effect) · Paul (name)

paltry (few) · poultry (fowl)

parish (diocese) · perish (die)

parlay (bet) · parley (talk)

parley (talk) · parlay (bet)

parole (prison) · payroll (pay)

partition (divider) · petition (plea)

passed (did pass) · past (former time)

passible (capable of feeling) · passable (capable of being passed)

pastoral (rural) · pastorale (music)

pastorale (music) · pastoral (rural)

pathos (tender) · bathos (anticlimax)

patience (forebearance) · patients (under doctor's care)

pause (delay) · paws (touch clumsily; feet) · pores (openings)

paw (foot) · pore (opening) · pour (make flow)

payroll (pay) · parole (prison)

peace (no war) · piece (portion)

peak (top) · pique (anger)

peaked (thin) · peeked (looked) · piqued (aroused)

peal (bell) · peel (strip)

pearl (gem) · purl (knitting)

pedal (foot lever) · peddle (sell)

peeked (looked) · peaked (thin) · piqued (aroused)

peer (look; equal) · pier (dock)

penance (religious) · pennants (sports)

pendant (ornament) · pendent (suspended)

pendent (suspended) · pendant (ornament)

pennants (sports) · penance (religious)

peon (peasant) · paean (hymn of joy)

perfect (exact) · prefect (high official)

perish (die) · parish (diocese)

persecute (to hound) · prosecute (enforce law)

personal (private) · personnel (employees)

perspective (vision) · prospective (future)

perverse (contrary) · preserve (save)

petition (plea) · partition (divider)

phantasy (same as *fantasy*, more archaic) · fantasy (a far-fetched imaginary idea)

phase (stage) · faze (worry) · fays (fairies)

phrase (words) · frays (battles)

phrenetic (insane) · frenetic (frantic)

physic (a remedy) · physique (body)

physical (body) · fiscal (money)

pica (printing measure) · piker (cheapskate)

117

picaresque (rascal) ·
picturesque (colorful)

picture (image) · pitcher
(vessel; baseball)

picturesque (colorful) ·
picaresque (rascal)

pidgin (the jargon used as a
language between foreigners
and the Chinese) · pigeon (a
bird) · piggin (a small wooden
pail)

piggin (a small wooden pail) ·
pigeon (a bird) · pidgin (the
jargon used as a language
between foreigners and the
Chinese)

piker (cheapskate) · pica
(printing measure)

pillar (column) · pillow (for
head)

pinnacle (peak) · pinochle
(game of cards)

pinochle (game of cards) ·
pinnacle (peak)

pious (religious) · Pius (name
of a Pope)

piqued (aroused) · peaked
(thin) · peeked (looked)

pistil (flower) · pistol (gun)

Pius (name of Pope) · pious
(religious)

plain (simple) · plane (smooth;
airplane)

plaintiff (one who sues) ·
plaintive (sad)

plait (braid) · plate (dish)

pleas (legal appeals) · please
(polite request)

plum (fruit) · plumb (line)

poker (cards) · polka (dance)

pole (tall wood) · poll (vote)

pore (opening; study) · pour
(with liquid)

poplar (tree) · popular (well-
known)

populace (the masses) ·
populous (thickly inhabited)

porpoise (mammal) · purpose
(aim)

portend (foretell) · pretend
(make believe)

portion (share) · potion (dose)

poultry (fowl) · paltry (few)

practice (the business of a
doctor) · practise (to repeat a
performance)

pray (say prayers) · prey
(victim)

precede (go before) · proceed
(advance)

precedence (priority of rank) ·
precedents (previous laws) ·
presidents (heads of state)

precedent (going before) ·
president (chief official)

precise (accurate) · precis
(resume)

precisian (a precise person) ·
precision (accuracy)

precision (accuracy) ·
precisian (a precise person)

prefect (high official) · perfect
(exact)

prefer (choose) · proffer
(offer)

preposition (grammar) ·
proposition (offer)

prescribe (give directions) ·
proscribe (to outlaw)

prescription (something
ordered) · proscription (an
imposed restriction)

presence (being present) ·
presents (plr. of verb: to
present; gifts)

presentiment (premonition) ·
presentment (presentation)

presents (plr. of verb: to
present; gifts) · presence
(being present)

118

preserve (save) · perverse (contrary)

president (chief official) · precedent (going before)

pretend (make-believe) · portend (foretell)

pries (opens) · prize (award)

prints (marks made by pressure) · prince (a title of nobility)

prodigy (young genius) · protégé (under care)

profit (gain) · prophet (one who predicts)

proscription (an imposed restriction) · prescription (something ordered)

prospective (future) · perspective (vision)

pubic (region of body) · public (people)

puny (slight) · puisne (a junior)

pupil (student) · pupal (development stage of larva)

purpose (aim) · porpoise (mammal)

put (place) · putt (golf)

Q

Incorrect	Correct	Incorrect	Correct
quafeur —	**coiffure**	questionaire ——	
qualefy ——	**qualify**		— **questionnaire**
quallity ——	**quality**	quier ——	**choir**
quanity —	**quantity**	quik ——	**quick**
quarel ——	**quarrel**	quivver ——	**quiver**
quarentine ——		quizes ——	**quizzes**
	— **quarantine**	quizical —	**quizzical**
quater ——	**quarter**		

Look-Alikes or Sound-Alikes

quarts (32 ounces) · **quartz** (a mineral)

quay (dock) · **key** (with lock)

quean (female cat; an immoral person) · **queen** (female sovereign)

queerest (strangest) · **querist** (questioner)

queue (line) · **cue** (hint; billiards)

quiet (still) · **quite** (completely, very)

quire (24 sheets) · **choir** (singers)

quote (saying) · **quota** (number)

R

Incorrect	Correct	Incorrect	Correct
rabees	rabies	rakoko	rococo
rable	rabble	rakontour	
rachit	ratchet		raconteur
racizm	racism	rakoon	raccoon
raddish	radish	ralie	rally
rade	raid	rambil	ramble
radicle	radical	rameedial	
radiel	radial		remedial
radient	radiant	rammafication	
radiod	radioed		ramification
radyis	radius	rammpage	
rafel	raffle		rampage
raff	raft	rampint	rampant
rafia	raffia	randim	random
raform	reform	rangle	wrangle
ragid	ragged	ranje	range
raglin	raglan	rankel	rankle
ragoo	ragout	rarety	rarity
rahtha	rather	ransid	rancid
railling	railing	ransome	ransom
raindeer	reindeer	rapayshus	
rainny	rainy		rapacious
raion	rayon	rapel	repel
raitable	ratable	rarly	rarely
raivin	raven	rashio	ratio
rajed	raged	rashnalize	
rakateer			rationalize
	racketeer	rashul	racial
raket	racket	rashun	ration
rakkish	rakish	rasser	razor

121

Incorrect	Correct	Incorrect	Correct
rasy	racy	recapichulate	
ratal	rattle		recapitulate
rath	wrath	recclamation	
rattlsnake			reclamation
	rattlesnake	reccomend	
raveel	reveal		recommend
ravije	ravage	recconoyter	
ravvil	ravel		reconnoiter
rawkus	raucous	reccord	record
rawr	raw	reccreation	
raydium	radium		recreation
rayment	raiment	reccumpense	
rayz	raze		recompense
rayzin	raisin	reccurrance	
razidjual	residual		recurrence
razzberry		receed	recede
	raspberry	receit	receipt
reakshun	reaction	recievable	
reakter	reactor		receivable
realaty	reality	recepy	recipe
realese	release	reces	recess
realise	realize	receshun	
realy	really		recession
reapper	reaper	recieve	receive
reaserch	research	reck	wreck
reath	wreath	recloose	recluse
reazon	reason	reconisonce	
rebell	rebel		reconnaissance
rebelyon	rebellion	reconize	
rebiuk	rebuke		recognize
rebutil	rebuttal	recooperate	
recalsatrate			recuperate
	recalcitrate	recovry	recovery

Incorrect	Correct	Incorrect	Correct
recquire	require	refrane	refrain
recrimnatory		refridgerator	
	recriminatory		refrigerator
recrute	recruit	refuzal	refusal
rectafy	rectify	regail	regale
rectul	rectal	reggard	regard
redemshun		regilate	regulate
	redemption	reglar	regular
reden	redden	regreshun	
rediculous			regression
	ridiculous	regretible	
redily	readily		regrettable
reduceable		regul	regal
	reducible	regurjatate	
redundent			regurgitate
	redundant	rehabbilitate	
reduse	reduce		rehabilitate
redy	ready	rehearsel	
reech	reach		rehearsal
reeder	reader	reherse	rehearse
reelizm	realism	rejament	regiment
reep	reap	rajecm	regime
referbish		rejensy	regency
	refurbish	rejeuvanate	
reffermation			rejuvenate
	reformation	rejon	region
reffugee	refugee	rejoyse	rejoice
refinment		rekin	reckon
	refinement	reklis	reckless
refleks	reflex	rekoop	recoup
reflekshun		rekord	record
	reflection	rektangul	
refrance	reference		rectangle

123

Incorrect	Correct	Incorrect	Correct
rekwital	requital	remnint	remnant
rekwizit	requisite	remoat	remote
relaition	relation	remonsterate	remonstrate
relaks	relax		
relavent	relevant	remoonerate	remunerate
releif	relief		
releive	relieve	remorsful	remorseful
relie	rely		
relient	reliant	removeable	removable
relinkwish	relinquish		
		removil	removal
relitive	relative	renagaid	renegade
rellegate	relegate	renaysense	renascence
rellish	relish		
relm	realm	rendevous	rendezvous
relucktinse	reluctance		
		reneg	renege
relyd	relied	renevate	renovate
relyible	reliable	renforce	reenforce
remane	remain		
reme	ream	renjin	Roentgen
remidy	remedy	rennasonse	renaissance
reminiss	reminisce		
		rentry	reentry
remishun	remission	renu	renew
		reorgenise	reorganize
remitant	remittent		
		reostat	rheostat
remitence	remittance	repare	repair
		repatishun	repetition
remmember	remember		
remmit	remit	repatory	repertory

124

Incorrect	Correct	Incorrect	Correct
repeel	repeal	repreive	reprieve
repelant		represed	
	repellent		repressed
reperbate		reprizal	reprisal
	reprobate	reprize	reprise
reperduce		reptil	reptile
	reproduce	rerite	rewrite
reperhensable		resadense	
	reprehensible		residence
repersent		resaleable	
	represent		resalable
repetative		resalution	
	repetitive		resolution
repete	repeat	reseption	
repeun	repugn		reception
replacment		resevation	
	replacement		reservation
replaka	replica	resevwar	
repleet	replete		reservoir
replie	reply	resind	rescind
repozatory		resint	recent
	repository	resipracal	
reppakushin			reciprocal
	repercussion	resiprosity	
reppatee	repartee		reciprocity
repport	report	resistence	
reppublican			resistance
	republican	resitashun	
repputible			recitation
	reputable	resle	wrestle
reprable	reparable	resorse	resource
repramand		resparator	
	reprimand		respirator

Incorrect	Correct	Incorrect	Correct
respectible		retuch	retouch
	respectable	revelle	reveille
respit	respite	revelution	
responsable			revolution
	responsible	revenew	revenue
resterant		revenje	revenge
	restaurant	revijun	revision
resteration		revilation	
	restoration		revelation
resumtion		revivle	revival
	resumption	revize	revise
resusitate		revokashun	
	resuscitate		revocation
resytul	recital	revrent	reverent
retale	retail	revult	revolt
retalliate	retaliate	revursible	
retane	retain		reversible
retch	wretch	revurt	revert
retier	retire	revvarie	reverie
retirment		reyn	rain
	retirement	rezanense	
retisent	reticent		resonance
retna	retina	rezemblence	
retorick	rhetoric		resemblance
retreive	retrieve	rezent	resent
retrosay	retroussé	rezerve	reserve
retrospeck		rezidew	residue
	retrospect	rezign	resign
rettribushun		rezilyens	
	retribution		resilience
rettrogreshun		rezin	resin
	retrogression	rezistable	
			resistible

Incorrect	Correct	Incorrect	Correct
rezistance ———		rime ———	**rhyme**
	— **resistance**	rince ———	**rinse**
reznable ———		rinestone ———	
	— **reasonable**		— **rhinestone**
rezolve ——	**resolve**	ringger ——	**ringer**
rezort ——	**resort**	rinkle ——	**wrinkle**
rezult ——	**result**	rinocerus ———	
rezume ——	**resume**		— **rhinoceros**
rezurecshun ———		rinseing ——	**rinsing**
	— **resurrection**	ripal ———	**ripple**
rhime ———	**rhyme**	rippen ——	**ripen**
rhythum —	**rhythm**	ripublic —	**republic**
ribben ——	**ribbon**	riquire ——	**require**
ribbuld ——	**ribald**	riseing ———	**rising**
ribin ———	**ribbon**	riskay ——	**risqué**
richous —	**righteous**	rist ———	**wrist**
richual ———	**ritual**	rithe ———	**writhe**
ridence —	**riddance**	rithem ——	**rhythm**
ridgid ———	**rigid**	ritten ——	**written**
ridul ———	**riddle**	riut ———	**riot**
rie ———	**rye**	rivel ———	**rival**
rifel ———	**rifle**	rivit ———	**rivet**
rigermarole ———		rize ———	**rise**
	— **rigmarole**	robbin ——	**robin**
rigerus —	**rigorous**	robery ——	**robbery**
rigur ———	**rigor**	Rockerfellow ———	
riht ———	**right**		— **Rockefeller**
rije ———	**ridge**	Rode Island ———	
Rik ———	**Reich**		— **Rhode Island**
rikity ——	**rickety**	rododendrum ———	
rikshaw —	**rickshaw**		— **rhododendron**
rilation —	**relation**	roebot ———	**robot**
rilegious —	**religious**	roge ———	**rogue**

Incorrect	Correct	Incorrect	Correct
rogish	roguish	ruder	rudder
roial	royal	ruf	rough
rok	rock	ruge	rouge
rokkit	rocket	ruller	ruler
rom	roam	rumatism	rheumatism
romanse	romance	rumba	rhumba
rong	wrong	rumbil	rumble
rooay	roué	rumer	rumor
rood	rude	rumije	rummage
roolet	roulette	rumy	rummy
roon	ruin	runer	runner
rooves	roofs	runing	running
roring	roaring	rupcher	rupture
rosery	rosary	rurel	rural
Rosevelt	Roosevelt	ruset	russet
rosey	rosy	Rusha	Russia
rost	roast	rusil	rustle
rotery	rotary	rustik	rustic
rotha	rather	rutine	routine
rotin	rotten	Ruzevelt	Roosevelt
roveing	roving	ryitus	riotous
royaly	royally	ryme	rhyme
roze	rose	rype	ripe
rozin	rosin	rythm	rhythm
rubarb	rhubarb		
ruber	rubber		

Look-Alikes or Sound-Alikes

rabbit (animal) · rarebit (food) · rabid (intense)

rain (water) · reign (rule) · rein (on horse)

raise (lift) · raze (demolish) · rays (light beams)

rap (knock) · wrap (fold)

rapped (knocked) · rapt (absorbed) · wrapped (packed)

read (book) · reed (grass) · red (color)

real (actual) · reel (wind in; stagger)

realize (understand) · relies (counts on)

rebate (deduction) · rebait (rehook)

rebound (to spring back) · redound (to accrue)

redound (to accrue) · rebound (to spring back)

reek (vapor) · wreak (inflict) · wreck (destroy)

referee (arbitrator) · reverie (dream)

relater (joiner) · relator (narrator)

relic (souvenir of the past) · relict (a widow)

respectfully (with esteem) · respectively (in the order given)

rest (repose) · wrest (pull away)

reveille (signal to awake) · revelry (gaiety)

reverend (minister) · reverent (respectful)

reverie (dream) · referee (arbitrator)

rhyme (poetry) · rhythm (meter, beat)

rhyme (verse) · rime (frost)

right (correct) · rite (ceremony) · wright (workman) · write (put words on paper)

rime (frost) · rhyme (verse)

ring (circle; bell) · wring (squeeze)

roam (wander) · Rome (city)

rock (stone; sway) · roc (fabled bird)

rode (past of ride) · road (path) · rowed (boat)

roe (doe, fish egg) · row (boating)

role (part) · roll (turn around; bread)

Rome (city) · roam (wander)

roomer (one who rooms) · rumor (gossip)

root (plant) · route (way of travel)

rose (flower) · rows (lines)

rote (mechanical repetition) · wrote (did write)

rough (coarse) · ruff (collar, fish; bluster)

rouse (awaken) · rows (quarrels)

rung (step; did ring) · wrung (squeezed)

rye (grain; alcohol) · wry (distorted)

129

S

Incorrect	Correct	Incorrect	Correct
Sabath —	Sabbath	sattelite —	satellite
sabbotage —		sattisfaction —	
	sabotage		satisfaction
sacarin —	saccharin	saught —	sought
sacerfice —	sacrifice	sausidge —	sausage
sacerment —		saveing —	saving
	sacrament	Sawk vaccine —	
sacreligous —			Salk vaccine
	sacrilegious	sayed —	said
safire —	sapphire	scarcly —	scarcely
safty —	safety	scarsity —	scarcity
sakred —	sacred	scedule —	schedule
sakrifice —	sacrifice	sceinse —	science
salammi —	salami	sceleton —	skeleton
salery —	salary	sceme —	scheme
sallary —	salary	scenry —	scenery
salm —	psalm	sceptical —	
sammon —	salmon		skeptical
sanatashun —		scithe —	scythe
	sanitation	scizzers —	scissors
sandwidge —		scolastic —	
	sandwich		scholastic
sargent —	sergeant	scool —	school
sarkastic —	sarcastic	Scripchure —	
sassiety —	society		Scripture
sassparilla —		seceed —	secede
	sarsaparilla	secertery —	
Sataday —	Saturday		secretary
satasfactory —		seduse —	seduce
	satisfactory	seedan —	sedan

130

Incorrect	Correct	Incorrect	Correct
seelect ——	select	sentor ——	centaur
seeries ——	series	sentury ——	century
seeson ——	season	senyer ——	senior
segragate ——		seperate —	separate
	segregate	sereal ——	cereal
seige ——	siege	sereise ——	series
seing ——	seeing	serface ——	surface
seive ——	sieve	sergery —	surgery
sekret ——	secret	serjon ——	surgeon
seldem —	seldom	sermen ——	sermon
selebrait ——		sermize ——	surmise
	celebrate	serplus ——	surplus
selery ——	celery	serprize —	surprise
seleschul —	celestial	sertificate ——	
selfs ——	selves		certificate
selibacy —	celibacy	servalanse ——	
sellar ——	cellar		surveillance
sellfish ——	selfish	servay ——	survey
selluloid ——		servicable ——	
	celluloid		serviceable
seme ——	seem	servise ——	service
sement —	cement	servive ——	survive
semetary ——		seseed ——	secede
	cemetery	sesession ——	
semmester ——			secession
	semester	Setember ——	
senater —	senator		September
sene ——	scene	sety ——	settee
senic ——	scenic	seudo ——	pseudo
sensative ——		seudonym ——	
	sensitive		pseudonym
sentenial ——		sivinth ——	seventh
	centennial	sevral ——	several

Incorrect	Correct	Incorrect	Correct
sexsy	sexy	shevron	
sez	says		chevron
shagrin	chagrin	shez	chaise
shaley	chalet	Shicago	Chicago
shampain		shicanery	
	champagne		chicanery
shamy	chamois	shiek	sheik
shandaleir		shiffon	chiffon
	chandelier	shillaylee	
shaperone			shillelagh
	chaperon	shineing	shining
shapo	chapeau	shipd	shipped
sharade	charade	shippment	
sharaid	charade		shipment
sharlatin		shoffer	
	charlatan		chauffeur
sharliton		sholders	
	charlatan		shoulders
shartroose		shoodn't	
	chartreuse		shouldn't
shartrus		shouldent	
	chartreuse		shouldn't
shato	château	showvinizm	
shef	chef		chauvinism
sheild	shield	shreik	shriek
sheke	chic	shrubry	
shelfs	shelves		shrubbery
sheneel	chenille	shud	should
shenyon	chignon	shugar	sugar
sheperd	shepherd	shure	sure
sherbert	sherbet	shuv	shove
sherif	sheriff	sience	science
sheth	sheath	sieze	seize

Look-Alikes or Sound-Alikes

sac (baglike part of animal or plant) · **sack** (bag)

sail (on boat) · **sale** (sell at low price)

salvage (to save from wreckage) · **selvage** (the edge of woven fabric)

sanitary (hygienic) · **sanitory** (conducive to health)

Satan (devil) · **satin** (fabric) · **sateen** (cotton fabric resembling satin)

satire (wit used to ridicule) · **satyr** (a sylvan deity or demigod)

savior (one who saves) · **Saviour** (Christ)

scene (place) · **seen** (did see)

scents (smells) · **sense** (brains) · **cents** (money)

schilling (German coin) · **shilling** (British coin)

scrip (money) · **script** (story)

sculptor (one who carves) · **sculpture** (work of sculptor)

sea (water) · **see** (vision)

sealing (closing) · **ceiling** (top of room)

seam (line) · **seem** (appear)

sear (burn) · **seer** (prophet)

seas (bodies of water) · **seize** (grab) · **sees** (observes)

seed (flower) · **cede** (give up)

sell (opposite of buy) · **cell** (prison; in biology)

seller (one who sells) · **cellar** (basement)

selvage (the edge of woven fabric) · **salvage** (to save from wreckage)

senior (older) · **señor** (mister)

senses (sight, touch) · **census** (population count)

serf (slave) · **surf** (sea)

serge (fabric) · **surge** (swell)

serial (in a row) · **cereal** (food)

session (meeting) · **cession** (yielding)

settler (colonist) · **settlor** (one who makes a legal settlement)

sew (stitch) · **so** (like this) · **sow** (plant)

shear (clip) · **sheer** (thin)

sheik (Arab chief) · **chic** (stylish)

sheriff (county officer) · **sheri** (Arab prince)

shilling (British coin) · **schilling** (German coin)

shirt (garment) · **chert** (a rock)

shoe (foot) · **shoo** (go away)

shone (did shine) · **shown** (did show)

shoot (fire) · **chute** (drop)

shriek (cry out) · **shrike** (bird)

sic (thus) · **sick** (ill)

Sicilian (from Sicily, an island off and part of Italy) · **Cilician** (from Cilicia, a province in Asia Minor)

side (next to) · **sighed** (did sigh)

sighs (sound) · **size** (bigness)

sight (see) · **site** (place) · **cite** (point out)

sign (symbol; put name on) · **sine** (mathematics)

signet (a seal) · **cygnet** (a young swan)

singeing (burning) · **singing** (song)

singing (song) · **singeing** (burning)

skull (head) · **scull** (boat)

slave (one who has lost his freedom) · **Slav** (one who speaks a Slavic language as his native tongue)

136

Incorrect	Correct	Incorrect	Correct
sigar	cigar	sinsere	sincere
sigarette		sinthetic	synthetic
	cigarette	sipher	cipher
siggnificant		siramics	ceramics
	significant	sircumstance	
signerture			circumstance
	signature	sirrup	syrup
sikada	cicada	sirynge	syringe
silance	silence	sisors	scissors
sillable	syllable	sist	cyst
sillabus	syllabus	sistem	system
silouette		sistern	cistern
	silhouette	sitadel	citadel
simbal	symbol	sittuation	
simester			situation
	semester	sixt	sixth
simetry		sizm	schism
	symmetry	skarce	scarce
similer	similar	skare	scare
simpathy		skedule	schedule
	sympathy	skeme	scheme
simphony		skism	schism
	symphony	skool	school
simton	symptom	skooner	schooner
sinamin		slayed	slain
	cinnamon	slax	slacks
sincerly	sincerely	sodder	solder
sinch	cinch	sofemore	
sinder	cinder		sophomore
sindicate		sofen	soften
	syndicate	sofer	sofa
sinnic	cynic	sofisticate	
sinse	since		sophisticate

133

Incorrect	Correct	Incorrect	Correct
solem	**solemn**	stateing	**stating**
soler	**solar**	statis	**status**
sollid	**solid**	statment	**statement**
sophmore		stattistic	**statistic**
	sophomore	stawk	**stalk**
sorce	**source**	stedy	**steady**
sord	**sword**	stelthy	**stealthy**
sorow	**sorrow**	stomick	**stomach**
sory	**sorry**	stoped	**stopped**
soshalist	**socialist**	storey	**story**
sosiety	**society**	straight-jacket	
sothern	**southern**		**— strait jacket**
sourkraut		strech	**stretch**
	— sauerkraut	strenth	**strength**
sovrin	**sovereign**	strenuoussly	
Sowvyet Union			**— strenuously**
	— Soviet Union	strenyous	
spagetti			**— strenuous**
	— spaghetti	stricly	**strictly**
Spanyerd		strugle	**struggle**
	— Spaniard	studdy	**study**
speach	**speech**	studeying	
speshialty			**— studying**
	— specialty	stuped	**stupid**
speshul	**special**	subburban	
spesify	**specify**		**— suburban**
spesiman		suberb	**suburb**
	— specimen	subordnate	
spirrit	**spirit**		**— subordinate**
sponser	**sponsor**	subscribtion	
sprily	**spryly**		**— subscription**
starberd		subsistance	
	— starboard		**— subsistence**

Incorrect	Correct	Incorrect	Correct
succede	**succeed**	supprise	**surprise**
succeser		supress	**suppress**
	— successor	suprintendent	
sucsess	**success**		**— superintendent**
sufferage	**suffrage**	suround	**surround**
suffishent		survise	**service**
	— sufficient	suspishon	
suficient			**— suspicion**
	— sufficient	sutle	**subtle**
sufix	**suffix**	suvenir	**souvenir**
suger	**sugar**	suvvival	**survival**
sugjest	**suggest**	swade	**suede**
sujjest	**suggest**	swair	**swear**
sujjestion		swave	**suave**
	— suggestion	syche	**psyche**
suksinct	**succinct**	sychiatrist	
sumary			**— psychiatrist**
	— summary	sychic	**psychic**
summarine		sychology	
	— submarine		**— psychology**
supena	**subpoena**	sychosis	
supercede			**— psychosis**
	— supersede	sygnificant	
suply	**supply**		**— significant**
supose	**suppose**	symetrical	
supperfluous			**— symmetrical**
	— superfluous	symtom	**symptom**
supplys	**supplies**	synic	**cynic**

slay (kill) · sleigh (sled)

sleight (trick) · slight (small; snub)

sloe (plum) · slow (not fast)

soar (rise) · sore (aching)

sodality (a fellowship) · solidarity (union)

sold (did sell) · soled (put on a sole)

soldier (military) · solder (to fuse)

sole (shoe) · soul (spirit)

some (a few) · sum (total)

someone (some person) · some one (one of several)

son (child) · sun (sky)

special (particular, specific) · especial (exceptional, preeminent)

specialty (an employment limited to one kind of work) · speciality (quality of being special)

specie (coin) · species (variety)

staid (sober) · stayed (remained)

stair (to climb) · stare (look steadily)

stake (post or gamble) · steak (food)

stalk (stem of plant; walk stealthily) · stork (bird)

stationary (fixed) · stationery (paper supplies)

statue (likeness) · stature (height) · statute (law)

steal (rob) · steel (metal)

step (pace) · steppe (plain)

stile (step) · style (fashion)

stork (bird) · stalk (stem of plant; walk stealthily)

straight (direct) · strait (body of water)

stricture (binding) · structure (form)

structure (form) · stricture (binding)

style (fashion) · stile (step)

suburb (near city) · superb (very good)

succor (help) · sucker (fool)

suit (clothes) · suite (rooms) · sweet (sugary)

sum (total) · some (a few)

summary (wrap-up) · summery (fit for summer)

sundae (ice-cream) · Sunday (Sabbath)

superb (very good) · suburb (near city)

symbol (sign) · cymbal (music)

T

Incorrect	Correct	Incorrect	Correct
tabblet	**tablet**	tecksture	**texture**
tabbulate		tecnical	**technical**
	tabulate	teech	**teach**
tabu	**taboo**	teenadger	
tafeta	**taffeta**		**teenager**
tailer	**tailor**	teen's	**teens**
tamata	**tomato**	teer	**tier**
tante	**taint**	teerful	**tearful**
takeing	**taking**	tejious	**tedious**
takkle	**tackle**	tekela	**tequila**
takt	**tact**	teknik	**technique**
taktics	**tactics**	tekstile	**textile**
tallent	**talent**	telagram	
tangable	**tangible**		**telegram**
tanjent	**tangent**	telavision	
tanntalize			**television**
	tantalize	tellephone	
tanntrum			**telephone**
	tantrum	tellevision	
targit	**target**		**television**
tarrif	**tariff**	temmerity	
tarrnish	**tarnish**		**temerity**
tassit	**tacit**	temmplit	
tasteing	**tasting**		**template**
tatered	**tattered**	temp	**tempt**
tatle	**tattle**	temperarily	
tatoo	**tattoo**		**temporarily**
taudry	**tawdry**	temperment	
teara	**tiara**		**temperament**

Incorrect	Correct	Incorrect	Correct
temprary		teratory	**territory**
	— temporary	terestrial	
temprature			**— terrestrial**
	— temperature	terible	**terrible**
temprence		terific	**terrific**
	— temperance	terify	**terrify**
temt	**tempt**	teritorial	
temtation			**— territorial**
	— temptation	terpentine	
tenament			**— turpentine**
	— tenement	terpitude	**turpitude**
tenasity	**tenacity**	terrer	**terror**
tendancy		terribally	**terribly**
	— tendency	testafy	**testify**
tenden	**tendon**	testamony	
tenent	**tenant**		**— testimony**
tener	**tenor**	testiment	
Tenesee			**— testament**
	— Tennessee	Teusday	**Tuesday**
tenible	**tenable**	texbook	**textbook**
tenit	**tenet**	theem	**theme**
tennacious		theeology	
	— tenacious		**— theology**
tenndenshous		theerum	**theorem**
	— tendentious	thef	**theft**
tennsion	**tension**	theif	**thief**
tennuous	**tenuous**	their's	**theirs**
tenticle	**tentacle**	theirselves	
tentitive	**tentative**		**— themselves**
teppee	**tepee**	theiter	**theater**
teppid	**tepid**	themselfs	
terane	**terrain**		**— themselves**

Incorrect	Correct	Incorrect	Correct
theriputic	— therapeutic	til	till
thermanooklear	— thermonuclear	timerity	temerity
thermistat	— thermostat	timmerous	— timorous
thersty	thirsty	timmid	timid
therteen	thirteen	tiney	tiny
thery	theory	tingel	tingle
thesirus	— thesaurus	tinn	tin
thesus	thesis	tinnsel	tinsel
theze	these	tipe	type
thiefs	thieves	tippoff	tip-off
thogh	though	tirant	tyrant
thoro	thorough	tirms	terms
thousind	— thousand	tite	tight
thred	thread	tittalate	titillate
threshhold	— threshold	tittle	title
thret	threat	tittular	titular
thriftey	thrifty	tobbaco	tobacco
thriling	thrilling	tobogun	—toboggan
thriveing	thriving	to-day	today
throte	throat	todey	toady
thugg	thug	togga	toga
thum	thumb	toggether	— together
thwort	thwart	toilit	toilet
Thyland	— Thailand	tokin	token
tickel	tickle	tole	toll
tieing	tying	tollerant	tolerant
		tomaine	— ptomaine
		tommorow	— tomorrow

Incorrect	Correct	Incorrect	Correct
tomoroe	— tomorrow	traser — tracer	
tonage — tonnage		trechery	— treachery
tonnic — tonic		tresurer — treasurer	
tonnsil — tonsil		trimendous	— tremendous
tonsalectomey	— tonsillectomy	tripplecate	— triplicate
toomstone	— tombstone	trist — tryst	
toogether	— together	truble — trouble	
		truefully	— truthfully
toolip — tulip		truely — truly	
toom — tomb		Trueman — Truman	
toonight — tonight		tryed — tried	
toor — tour		tryumph — triumph	
Toosday — Tuesday		tummul — tumult	
toothe — tooth		tung — tongue	
topick — topic		tunnage — tonnage	
toppic — topic		turminate	— terminate
tora — Torah		turminel — terminal	
torador — toreador		turmite — termite	
torement — torment		turms — terms	
torenado — tornado		turse — terse	
torepedo — torpedo		twealth — twelfth	
torid — torrid		twelth — twelfth	
torint — torrent		tympany — timpani	
tork — torque		typeriter	— typewriter
torper — torpor		tyrade — tirade	
totling — totaling		tythe — tithe	
tousand — thousand		Tywan — Taiwan	
tradegy — tragedy			
transferr — transfer			
transsfer — transfer			

Look-Alikes or Sound-Alikes

tacked (fastened) · **tact** (consideration)

tacks (fasteners) · **tax** (money paid government)

tail (end) · **tale** (story)

talc (powder) · **talk** (speak)

taper (candle; narrow) · **tapir** (animal)

tarantella (dance) · **tarantula** (spider)

tare (weight) · **tear** (rip)

tartar (on teeth; chemical) · **tartare** (sauce) · **Tatar** (a people) · **Tartar** (a people)

taught (did teach) · **taut** (tense)

tax (money paid government) · **tacks** (fasteners)

team (group) · **teem** (swarm)

tear (crying) · **tier** (layer)

teas (drinks) · **tease** (annoy)

technics (technical rules) · **techniques** (manners of performance)

techniques (manners of performance) · **technics** (technical rules)

teeth (plural of tooth) · **teethe** (to grow teeth)

tenant (renter) · **tenet** (belief)

tenor (singer) · **tenure** (duration)

tern (bird) · **turn** (rotate)

than (as in "greater than") · **then** (at that time)

their (belong to them) · **there** (that place) · **they're** (they are)

thence (from that time or place) · **hence** (from this time or place)

therefor (for that, for it, for them, etc.) · **therefore** (for this reason)

therefore (for this reason) · **therefor** (for that, for it, for them, etc.)

thrash (to swing or strike) · **thresh** (to beat out grain)

threw (tossed) · **through** (penetrated; finished)

throe (pang) · **throw** (hurl)

throne (king) · **thrown** (tossed)

throw (hurl) · **throe** (pang)

tic (twitching) · **tick** (pillow; clock)

tide (ocean) · **tied** (connected)

timber (wood) · **timbre** (tone)

tinny (like tin) · **tiny** (small)

tiny (small) · **tinny** (like tin)

to (toward) · **too** (also) · **two** (number)

toe (foot) · **tow** (pull)

toiled (worked) · **told** (said)

toilet (bathroom) · **toilette** (grooming, attire)

told (said) · **toiled** (worked)

tomb (grave) · **tome** (book)

tongue (in mouth) · **tong** (weapon)

topee (sun-helmet) · **toupee** (hairpiece for men)

topography (maps, charts) · **typography** (printing)

tortious (legal term referring to tort) · **tortuous** (twisting) · **torturous** (painful)

toupee (hairpiece for men) · **topee** (sun-helmet)

tour (trip) · **tower** (building)

track (path) · **tract** (region)

trail (path) · **trial** (court)

treaties (agreements) · **treatise** (account)

troop (company of soldiers) · **troupe** (company of actors)

tuba (musical instrument) · **tuber** (root of plant)

turban (hat) · **turbine** (power)

typography (printing) · **topography** (maps, charts)

U

Incorrect	Correct	Incorrect	Correct
ubbiquitous	——	unason	—— **unison**
	— **ubiquitous**	Unatarian	——
ucharist	——		— **Unitarian**
	— **Eucharist**	unatural	——
uge	—— **huge**		— **unnatural**
ugenics	— **eugenics**	unaverse	——
ukalalee	— **ukulele**		— **universe**
ulltimite	— **ultimate**	unawganized	——
ulltirior	— **ulterior**		— **unorganized**
ulogy	—— **eulogy**	unconsolable	——
ulser	—— **ulcer**		— **inconsolable**
ultamatum	——	undaprivilledged	—
	— **ultimatum**		— **underprivileged**
umane	— **humane**	undataker	——
umberella	——		— **undertaker**
	— **umbrella**	unddress	— **undress**
umble	— **humble**	undeground	——
umbridge	——		— **underground**
	— **umbrage**	underiter	——
umility	— **humility**		— **underwriter**
ummbillical	——	underrite	——
	— **umbilical**		— **underwrite**
ummpire	— **umpire**	undigestible	——
umpopular	——		— **indigestible**
	— **unpopular**	undinyable	——
unalatteral	——		— **undeniable**
	— **unilateral**	undisirable	——
unamed	— **unnamed**		— **undesirable**
unanamus	——	undoo	—— **undue**
	— **unanimous**	undoubtably	——
			— **undoubtedly**

Incorrect	Correct	Incorrect	Correct
unduely	unduly	unholey	unholy
undyeing		unick	eunuch
	undying	unifey	unify
uneek	unique	uniquivikal	
uneiform	uniform		unequivocal
unempeachible		unitey	unity
	unimpeachable	Unitid Stats	
unerned			United States
	unearned	univercity	
unerth	unearth		university
unescapable		universly	
	inescapable		universally
unesessary		unkemp	unkempt
	unnecessary	unkle	uncle
unezy	uneasy	unkonditionel	
unfagetible			unconditional
	unforgettable	unkonscious	
unfare	unfair		unconscious
unfinnished		unkooth	uncouth
	unfinished	unkshus	unctuous
unfitt	unfit	unncommon	
unfotunate			uncommon
	unfortunate	unneqil	unequal
unfrendly		unnering	unerring
	unfriendly	unnerstand	
unfrequent			understand
	infrequent	unnfavrable	
ungoddly			unfavorable
	ungodly	unnit	unit
ungreatful		Unnited Nashuns	
	ungrateful		United Nations
unhelthy		unnocupied	
	unhealthy		unoccupied

Incorrect	Correct	Incorrect	Correct
unnowable	———	unsertin	———
	— **unknowable**		— **uncertain**
unnpregudiced	——	untill	——— **until**
	— **unprejudiced**	unumployed	——
unnprincipaled	——		— **unemployed**
	— **unprincipled**	urb	——— **herb**
unplesent	———	useable	—— **usable**
	— **unpleasant**	usefull	—— **useful**
unpresidented	——	useing	—— **using**
	— **unprecedented**	use to	——— **used to**
unredeemable	———	usualy	—— **usually**
	— **irredeemable**		

Look-Alikes or Sound-Alikes

udder (part of cow) · utter (speak)

umpire (referee) · empire (dominion)

unable (not able) · enable (to make able)

unique (sole) · eunuch (sexless)

urn (vase) · earn (gain; to receive a salary)

utter (speak) · udder (part of a cow)

145

V

Incorrect	Correct	Incorrect	Correct
vaccilate —	**vacillate**	vegetible —	
vacinnation —			— **vegetable**
	— **vaccination**	vegitable —	
vacume —	**vacuum**		— **vegetable**
vakairo —	**vaquero**	vegitible —	
valer ———	**valor**		— **vegetable**
valintine —		vegitibul —	
	— **valentine**		— **vegetable**
vallid ———	**valid**	vehamint —	
valuble —	**valuable**		— **vehement**
valv ———	**valve**	vehimint —	
vanaty ———	**vanity**		— **vehement**
vandel ———	**vandal**	veicle ———	**vehicle**
vaneer ———	**veneer**	velosity —	**velocity**
vanesh ———	**vanish**	venam ———	**venom**
vannila ———	**vanilla**	Veneetion —	
vantrillokwist ———			— **Venetian**
	— **ventriloquist**	vengance —	
vantriloquist ———			— **vengeance**
	— **ventriloquist**	venil ———	**venal**
vaped ———	**vapid**	venim ———	**venom**
vassel ———	**vassal**	venimus —	
Vatecan —	**Vatican**		— **venomous**
vaze ———	**vase**	Veniss ———	**Venice**
veanul ———	**venal**	venorashun —	
vecablerry —			— **veneration**
	— **vocabulary**	venorible —	
vecks ———	**vex**		— **venerable**
vecter ———	**vector**	ventellacion —	
veenel ———	**venal**		— **ventilation**

146

Incorrect	**Correct**	Incorrect	**Correct**
ventellate	——	vermen ——	**vermin**
	— ventilate	vermooth	——
venttullation	——		**— vermouth**
	— ventilation	vermuth	——
ventullation	——		**— vermouth**
	— ventilation	vernackuler	——
venul ——	**venal**		**— vernacular**
venum ——	**venom**	vernackulur	——
venumus	——		**— vernacular**
	— venomous	versafy ——	**versify**
verafiable	——	versas ——	**versus**
	— verifiable	versefacation	——
verafucation	——		**— versification**
	— verification	versefecation	——
verafy ——	**verify**		**— versification**
verafyible	——	versifucation	——
	— verifiable		**— versification**
veraly ——	**verily**	versitil —	**versatile**
verassity	——	versufy ——	**versify**
	— veracity	versutil —	**versatile**
veraty ——	**verity**	vertabra —	**vertebra**
verbil ——	**verbal**	vertabrate	——
verbily ——	**verbally**		**— vertebrate**
verble ——	**verbal**	vertabril	——
verbul ——	**verbal**		**— vertebral**
verbully —	**verbally**	vertibrate	——
verchu ——	**virtue**		**— vertebrate**
vergin ——	**virgin**	vertibrul	——
veriaty ——	**variety**		**— vertebral**
verible —	**variable**	verticle —	**vertical**
verilaty ——	**virility**	vertiu ——	**virtue**
verious ——	**various**	vertubra —	**vertebra**
verius ——	**various**	vertue ——	**virtue**

147

Incorrect	Correct	Incorrect	Correct
verufyible	— verifiable	victum	victim
veruly	verily	vieing	vying
veruty	verity	viel	veil
veryous	various	vien	vein
vesinety	vicinity	vigar	vigor
vesle	vessel	vigel	vigil
vessal	vessel	vigelence	— vigilance
vessul	vessel	viger	vigor
vestabule	— vestibule	vigerous	vigorous
		vigur	vigor
vestabyul	— vestibule	vilage	village
		vilense	violence
vestad	vested	villege	village
vestage	vestige	vilet	violet
vestid	vested	villify	vilify
vestitch	vestige	villige	village
vestubyule	— vestibule	villin	villain
		vinager	vinegar
vetaranery	— veterinary	vindacate	— vindicate
veterinery	— veterinary	vindecate	— vindicate
Vet Nam	— Viet Nam	vinear	veneer
		vineer	veneer
vetos	vetoes	vinella	vanilla
vetrans	veterans	violon	violin
vibrent	vibrant	vipar	viper
vibrunt	vibrant	vipur	viper
victam	victim	virtebrate	— vertebrate
victem	victim		
victer	victor	virulance	— virulence
victom	victim		
victry	victory	virulant	virulent

148

Incorrect	Correct	Incorrect	Correct
virulunt	**virulent**	volyum	**volume**
viscious	**vicious**	vomet	**vomit**
vise	**vice**	vomut	**vomit**
visiate	**vitiate**	vosiferus	
visige	**visage**		**vociferous**
visinnity	**vicinity**	voyce	**voice**
visuge	**visage**	voys	**voice**
vitaman	**vitamin**	vulger	**vulgar**
vitel	**vital**	vuntrilloquist	
vitelly	**vitally**		**ventriloquist**
vitely	**vitally**	vurnaculer	
vitle	**vital**		**vernacular**
vittles	**victuals**	vurs	**verse**
vitul	**vital**	vursatil	**versatile**
vitully	**vitally**	vurses	**versus**
viuble	**viable**	vursifucation	
viubul	**viable**		**versification**
vivad	**vivid**	vursus	**versus**
vivod	**vivid**	vurtabra	**vertebra**
vizable	**visible**	vurtue	**virtue**
vodvil	**vaudeville**	vusinaty	**vicinity**
volentary		vyabel	**viable**
	voluntary		

Look-Alikes or Sound-Alikes

vacation (rest) · vocation (job)

vain (proud) · vane (weather) · vein (blood)

valance (drapery) · valence (in chemistry, degree of combining power)

vale (valley) · veil (face covering)

valence (in chemistry, degree of combining power) · valance (drapery)

veracity (truth) · voracity (hunger)

veracious (truthful) · voracious (greedy)

verses (poetry) · versus (against)

veto (vote no) · Vito (name)

vial (glass) · vile (loathsome) · viol (music)

vice (depraved) · vise (hold)

Volga (Russian river) · vulgar (crude, impolite)

voracity (hunger) · veracity (truth)

W

Incorrect	Correct	Incorrect	Correct
wafur	wafer	werld	world
waggon	wagon	wership	worship
wakon	waken	werth	worth
wakun	waken	wery	wary
wallnut	walnut	westurn	western
wallut	wallet	wether	weather
wantin	wanton	wether	whether
wantun	wanton	whisle	whistle
warbel	warble	wiald	wild
warbil	warble	wickad	wicked
warbul	warble	wickud	wicked
wardan	warden	wield	wild
wardon	warden	wierd	weird
wardun	warden	wifes	wives
warrantee		wilderniss	
	warranty		wilderness
warreor	warrior	wildurnes	
warriur	warrior		wilderness
waryer	warrior	wildurniss	
wasteage	wastage		wilderness
waylayed	waylaid	wile	while
wearhouse		wimmen	women
	warehouse	wins	wince
weary	wary	winse	wince
weding	wedding	wipperwill	
wellcome	welcome		whippoorwill
wellfare	welfare	Wisconson	
welth	wealth		Wisconsin
Wensday		wisedom	wisdom
	Wednesday	wisk broom	
weppon	weapon		whisk broom

Incorrect	Correct	Incorrect	Correct
wisky	whiskey	woom	womb
wisper	whisper	woosted	worsted
wite	white	worning	warning
withar	wither	worp	warp
withold	withhold	wossel	wassail
withur	wither	wot	what
wiuld	wild	wresle	wrestle
wizzard	wizard	writeing	writing
wolfs	wolves	wun	won
wonderous		wund	wound
	wondrous	wurld	world
wonst	once	wurm	worm

Look-Alikes or Sound-Alikes

wade (walk through water) · weighed (did weigh)

wail (cry) · whale (mammal)

waist (body) · waste (unused)

wait (stay for) · weight (heaviness)

waive (give up) · wave (water; gesture)

waiver (surrender claim) · waver (falter)

war (combat) · wore (past tense of wear)

ward (hospital) · warred (fought)

ware (goods) · wear (clothes) · where (which place?)

way (direction) · weigh (pounds) · whey (milk)

we (us) · wee (tiny)

weak (feeble) · week (7 days)

weal (state) · we'll (we will)

wheel (round body)

weather (atmosphere) · whether (if)

welch (cheat) · Welsh (from Wales)

wet (water) · whet (appetite)

which (what one?) · witch (hag)

Whig (political party) · wig (hair)

while (during) · wile (trick)

whine (complain) · wine (drink)

whither (where) · wither (decay)

whole (complete) · hole (opening)

wholly (fully) · holey (having holes) · holy (religious)

whoop (holler) · hoop (circle)

who's (who is) · whose (to whom)

won (did win) · one (single)

wont (habit) · won't (will not)

wood (lumber) · would (might)

wore (past tense of wear) · war (combat)

wrap (fold) · rap (knock)

wrapped (packed) · rapt (absorbed) · rapped (knocked)

wreak (inflict) · wreck (destroy) · reek (vapor)

wrest (pull away) · rest (repose)

wretch (louse) · retch (vomit)

wright (workman) · write (put words on paper) · right (correct) · rite (ceremony)

wring (squeeze) · ring (circle; bell)

wrote (did write) · rote (mechanical repetition)

wrung (squeezed) · rung (step; did ring)

wry (distorted) · rye (grain; alcohol)

XYZ

Incorrect	Correct	Incorrect	Correct
xlyaphone		yondur	yonder
	xylophone	youngstor	
Xmass	Xmas		youngster
y'all	you all	youngstur	
yat	yacht		youngster
yeild	yield	your's	yours
yeller	yellow	yungster	
Yeman	Yemen		youngster
yerself	yourself	Zar	Czar
yestaday		Zavier	Xavier
	yesterday	zeel	zeal
yestiday		zeenith	zenith
	yesterday	zefir	zephyr
yesturday		zefur	zephyr
	yesterday	zepher	zephyr
yodal	yodel	zink	zinc
yogart	yogurt	zithar	zither
	(or: yoghurt)	zithur	zither
yogee	yogi	zodeac	zodiac
yogert	yogurt	zoolegy	zoology
	(or: yoghurt)	Zus	Zeus
yogu	yoga	Zuse	Zeus
yoman	yeoman	zylophone	
yondar	yonder		xylophone

154

Look-Alikes or Sound-Alikes

yawl (sailboat) · yowl (loud cry)

yaws (tropical disease) · yours (possessive of you)

yew (tree) · you (person) · ewe (sheep)

yoke (frame for animals) · yolk (egg)

you'll (you will) · **Yule** (Christmas)

your (belongs to you) · you're (you are)

yours (possessive of you) · yaws (tropical disease)

yowl (loud cry) · yawl (sailboat)

QUICK LIST OF
CORRECT SPELLINGS

aardvark
Aaron
abandon
abbreviate
abdomen
ability
abolition
abrupt
absence
absent
absolutely
absurd
abuse
abyss
academic
accede
accelerate
accent
access
accessory
accident
accidentally
acclaim
acclimate
accommodate
accompany
accomplice
accomplish
accord
according
accordion
accost
account
accountant
accredit
accrue
accumulate
accuracy

accurate
accuse
accustom
ace
ache
achieve
acid
acknowledge
acknowledg-
  ment
acne
acoustics
acquaintance
acquire
acquisition
acquit
acquittal
acre
acreage
acrobat
across
acrostic
actor
actual
actually
acumen
acute
adage
adamant
addict
addition
address
Adenauer
adequate
adequately
adhere
adjacent
adjourn

adjustable
adjutant
administra-
  tion
administrator
admirable
admiral
admissible
admission
admit
admittance
adolescence
adolescent
adopt
adorable
adult
advance
advantage
advantageous
advertise
advertise-
  ment
advisable
adviser
advisory
advocate
aerial
aerodynamics
aeronautics
aerosol
affable
affair
affect
affidavit
affiliate
affirm
affix
afflict

affluence
afford
affront
Afghan
afraid
Africa
afterwards
against
aged
agencies
agency
agenda
aggrandize
aggravate
aggregate
aggressive
aghast
aging
agrarian
agree
agreeable
agreeing
agriculture
aground
airplane
aisle
alcohol
alert
alibi
alien
align
allege
allegiance
allergy
alleviate
alley
alliance
allocate

aring
arnal
arnival
carouse
carriage
carried
carrot
carrying
carte blanche
cartel
cartilage
carton
cartoon
cartridge
cascade
casement
cashew
cashier
cashmere
casket
casserole
cassock
castanet
castigate
castle
casualty
cataclysm
catacomb
catalog
catapult
cataract
catarrh
catastrophe
catch
category
caterpillar
catholic
caucus
cauliflower
caulk
cause
caustic
caution

cavalcade
cavalier
cavernous
cease
cedar
ceiling
celebrate
celery
celestial
celibacy
cellar
cello
cellophane
celluloid
Celtic
cement
cemetery
census
centaur
centennial
central
centrifugal
century
ceramics
cereal
cerebral
ceremony
certain
certificate
chafe
chagrin
chagrined
chain
chair
chaise
chalet
chalk
challenge
chameleon
chamois
champagne
champion
chandelier

changeable
channel
chaos
chapéau
chaperon
chaplain
character
charade
chariot
charity
charlatan
chartreuse
chasm
chaste
château
chatter
chauffeur
chauvinism
cheap
cheat
cheese
Cheddar
chef
chemical
chemist
chenille
cherub
chestnut
Chevrolet
chevron
chic
Chicago
chicanery
chief
chieftain
chiffon
chignon
children
chimney
chinchilla
chintz
Chippendale
chiropody

chisel
chivalrous
chlorine
chloroform
chocolate
choice
choir
cholera
choreography
chorus
chosen
chow mein
christen
Christian
Christmas
chromatism
chrome
chronic
chrysanthe-
mum
chubby
chummy
cicada
cider
cigar
cigarette
cinch
Cincinnati
cinder
cinnamon
cipher
circle
circuit
circular
circumcise
circumferenc
circumstance
cistern
citadel
citation
citizen
citrus
civil

allot
alloting
allotment
allotted
allow
allowance
allowed
all right
ally
almanac
almighty
almond
almost
alone
alphabet
already
also
alternate
although
altogether
altruism
aluminum
always
amateur
ambassador
ambiguous
ambulance
ameliorate
amenable
amend
amendment
American
amiable
amity
ammonia
ammunition
among
amorous
amount
amour
amusement
analog
analogy

analysis
analyze
anatomy
ancestor
ancestry
anchor
anchovy
ancient
anecdote
anew
ankle
annex
annihilate
anniversary
annotate
announce-
ment
annoyance
annual
annually
annuity
annul
annulled
anoint
anonymous
another
answer
antarctic
antecedent
antenna
anti-
American
antibiotic
anticipate
antique
anxiety
anxious
any
any time
anywhere
apartment
aphorism
apologetically

apologies
apologize
apology
apostle
apostrophe
apparatus
apparel
apparent
apparently
appeal
appear
appearance
appease
appellate
appendec-
tomy
appendix
appetite
applaud
appliance
applicant
applies
apply
appoint
appointee
appraisal
appraise
appreciable
appreciate
apprehend
apprentice
apricot
approach
apropos
appropriate
approve
approximate
apron
aptitude
arbitrator
arbitrary
arbitrate
archaic

architect
archives
arctic
area
arguing
argument
arise
arising
arithmetic
Arkansas
armada
armful
armistice
around
arouse
arousing
arraign
arrange
arrangement
arrears
arrest
arrival
arrive
arrogant
arrow
artery
article
artificial
artillery
artistically
ascend
ascertain
ashen
Asia
asinine
asked
asphalt
aspirant
aspirin
assail
assassin
assassinate
assault

assemble
assent
assert
assess
asset
assign
assimilable
assist
assistance
assistant
associate
assort
assume
assurance
assure
asthma
astronaut
asylum
ate
atheist
athlete
athletic
atmosphere
attach
attack
attacked
attain
attempt
attend
attendance
attendant
attention
attest
attic
attire
attitude
attorney
attract
audible
audience
auditorium
August
au revoir

authentic
author
authority
authorize
automatic
automatically
automation
automobile
autumn
auxiliary
available
avalanche
average
aviator
avid
avoidable
awe
awful
awkward
axis
bacchanal
bachelor
background
backward
bacon
bade
badge
bagel
baggage
balance
balk
ballad
ballet
ballistics
ballot
balmy
banana
bandage
banister
banjos
bankrupt

bankruptcy
banner
baptize
barbecue
bargain
barley
barracks
barrage
barrel
barricade
basic
basically
basis
bastard
baste
battalion
battery
beacon
beautician
beautiful
beauty
beaver
because
become
becoming
beetle
before
began
beggar
begin
beginner
beginning
behavior
beige
belief
believe
belittle
belligerent
bely
beneath
beneficial
beneficiary
benefit

benefited
benevolent
bent
berate
berserk
besiege
bestial
betray
better
beware
beyond
Bible
biceps
bicycle
bier
bigamy
biggest
bigot
bilious
billet
billiard
billion
binary
binoculars
biography
birch
bird
birdie
biscuit
bisect
bitter
bivouac
blackguard
blameful
blameless
blanket
blare
blasé
blasphemy
bleach
bleak
blessed
blight

blithe
blitz
blizzard
block
blockade
blotter
blouse
bludgeon
bluff
board
boast
boatswain
body
boisterous
bolster
bomb
bonfire
bonnet
bonsoir
bonus
bony
bookkeeping
borrow
bosom
bossy
botch
bottle
bottom
boudoir
bought
bouillon
boulevard
boundary
bouquet
bourbon
bourgeois
boycott
bracelet
braggart
braid
brain
brake
brand-new

brassiere
bravery
breadth
breakable
breakfast
breast
breed
breeze
brethren
bridge
brief
brigadier
bright
brilliant
Britain
Britannica
broccoli
broken
brokerage
bronchial
brook
browse
bruise
bucket
buckle
Buddha
budge
budget
buffalo
buffer
buffet
buffoon
bugle
build
built
bulldozer
bullet
bulletin
bumblebee
bungalow
bunion
buoy
buoyant

burden
bureau
burglary
burial
bursar
burst
busily
business
bustle
busybody
button
buxom
cabbage
cabinet
cable
cache
cactus
cadet
café
caffeine
calamity
calcium
calendar
calf
caliber
calico
California
calisthenics
calk
calm
calves
calypso
calorie
camaraderie
camel
camellia
camera
camisole
camouflage
campaign
camphor

cam...
Cana...
canal
canapé
cancel
cancer
candidat...
candle
candor
canine
canister
canker
cannery
cannibal
cannon
canoe
canopy
cantaloup
cantilever
canvas
canyon
capable
capacious
capacity
capillary
capital
capitulate
caprice
capsule
captain
caption
carafe
caramel
carat
carbohydrate
carburetor
cardiac
cardinal
career
careful
caress
Caribbean
caricature

civilization
clairvoyance
clamor
clannish
claque
classify
clause
cleanse
clearance
cleavage
clerical
clientele
cliff
climb
clipper
clique
cloak
cloche
clock
cloister
closet
closure
clothes
clown
clumsy
coach
coercion
coffee
coffin
cogitate
cognac
coherent
coiffure
coincidence
coleslaw
colic
coliseum
collaborate
collapse
collapsible
collar
collateral
colleague

collect
collector
college
collegiate
collision
colloquial
colonel
colonnade
color
coloratura
cologne
colossal
Colosseum
column
columnist
comb
comedian
comedy
comet
comfortable
comic
coming
comma
command
commemorate
commendable
commensu-
    rate
commercial
commission
commit
committed
committee
commodity
common
communicate
communism
communist
community
commute
companion
comparable

comparative
compass
compatible
compel
compelled
compensation
compete
competence
competent
competition
complemen-
    tary
complexion
compliance
complicate
compose
composition
compressed
compromise
comptroller
compulsory
comrade
conceal
concede
conceit
conceive
concentrate
concentric
concept
concert
concession
conciliate
concise
conclave
concoct
concourse
concrete
concur
concurrence
concussion
condemn
condensation
condescend

condition
conduct
confectionary
confederate
conference
conferred
confess
confidence
confinement
confirm
conflagration
Confucius
congeal
congenial
congratulate
congregation
congruous
conjecture
conjugate
conjure
connect
Connecticut
connection
connoisseur
connotation
connote
connubial
conquer
conscience
conscientious
conscious
consensus
consequence
conservatory
consider
considerable
consignment
consistent
console
consolidate
constable
constant
constellation

161

consul
consummate
consumption
contagious
contain
contemplate
contemporary
contempt
contemptible
continent
continually
continuous
contour
contractual
contrariwise
contrary
contretemps
contribute
control
controlled
controversial
convalesce
convenient
converge
converse
convertible
convolute
convulse
cookery
coolly
cooper
cooperate
coordination
Copenhagen
copious
copyright
copywriter
coral
cordage
cordial
corduroy
corkage
corned-beef

corner
cornice
coronary
coroner
corporal
corporation
corps
corpuscle
corral
corralled
correct
correlate
correspond
corridor
corroborate
corrugated
corrupt
corsage
corset
cosmic
cosmopolitan
Cossack
cotillion
cottage
cotton
cough
counselor
countenance
counterfeit
countess
country
coup
de grace
coupé
couple
coupon
courage
course
court
courteous
courtesan
courtesy
courtmartial

cousin
covenant
cover
coverage
coward
coxswain
coyly
coyote
cozy
crabby
crack
crackle
cradle
craft
cranberry
crane
crawl
crayon
cream
crease
creation
creature
credence
credential
credible
credulous
crepe
crescendo
crew
cricket
cried
criminal
crimson
cripple
critical
criticize
critique
crochet
crocodile
croquet
croquette
croupier
crowd

crowned
crucial
crude
cruel
cruelly
cruelty
cruiser
crumb
crutch
cry
cryptic
crystallize
Cuba
cuckoo
cudgel
culinary
culture
cunning
cupboard
curfew
curiosity
curious
curly
currency
current
curriculum
cursed
curtain
curve
custard
custody
customer
cultivate
cycle
cyclone
cylinder
cynic
cyst
Czar
Czecho-
slovakia

dabble	decorate	demonstrate	detergent
dachshund	decrease	denial	deteriorate
dacron	dedicate	dense	determine
daffodil	deduce	dental	deterrent
dagger	deductible	dentifrice	detestable
dahlia	default	dentist	deuce
daily	defeat	deny	devastate
daiquiri	defendant	deodorant	develop
dairy	defense	departure	device
damage	defensible	dependable	devil
dandelion	deference	dependent	devious
dandruff	deferred	deplete	devise
dangerous	defiance	deposit	devoid
data	deficient	depot	devotion
daughter	deficit	depravation	diabetes
dauphin	defied	deprecate	dextrous
dawdle	definite	depressant	diagnose
dazzle	definitely	deprivation	dialect
deacon	definition	deprive	diamond
dead	defy	depths	diaper
deaf	De Gaulle	deputy	diaphragm
dealt	dehydrate	derelict	diary
debate	deign	derive	dichotomy
debauchery	Delaware	derogative	dictionary
debonair	delegate	derrick	didn't
debris	deliberate	descend	die
debt	delicacy	describe	diesel
debut	delicatessen	description	dietary
decade	delicious	desecrate	dietitian
decease	delight	desegregate	difference
deceit	delinquent	desertion	differential
deceive	delivery	desiccate	difficult
December	deluge	design	diffuse
decent	delusion	desirable	digest
decibel	deluxe	desolate	digestible
decided	demagogue	despair	digging
deciduous	dementia	desperate	digitalis
decimal	praecox	despicable	digressive
decipher	demi-tasse	destination	dilapidate
decision	democracy	destroy	dilemma
declaration	democrat	destruction	diligent
decline	demolish	detail	dilute
décolleté	demonstrable	detect	dimension

163

diminish	disparage	divulge	dress
diminutive	dispensary	docile	dried
dinette	disperse	doctor	driftwood
dining	displacement	doctrinaire	drill
dinner	disposable	documentary	drink
dinosaur	disposal	dodge	drive-in
diocese	dispossess	does	driveway
diphtheria	disproportion	doggerel	drizzle
diploma	dispute	doldrums	droll
dire	disqualify	dollar	dromedary
direction	disreputable	dolphin	droop
dirge	disrupt	domicile	dropping
dirty	dissatisfy	dominant	drowned
disagreement	dissect	domineer	drowse
disallow	disseminate	dominion	drudgery
disappear	dissent	domino	druggist
disappoint	dissident	donkey	drunkenness
disapprobation	dissimilar	donor	dry
disarray	dissipate	don't	dual
disastrous	dissociate	doom	dubious
disbursement	dissolution	door	dulcet
discard	dissolve	dormant	dullness
discern	dissonant	dormitory	duly
disciple	dissuade	dosage	dumb
discipline	distaff	dossier	dunce
discommodity	distance	double	dungaree
disconcert	distasteful	doubt	dungeon
disconsolate	distillation	dough	duplex
discount	distinct	doughnut	duplicate
discourteous	distinguish	dove	duplicity
discover	distraught	dovetail	durable
discrepancy	distress	dowager	duration
discriminate	distribute	dowdy	duress
discuss	district	dowry	during
discussion	disturb	dozen	Dutch
disdain	ditto	dragon	dutiful
disease	divan	drainage	duty
disguise	diverge	drama	dwarf
dishonest	divert	drawn	dying
disillusion	divide	dread	dynamic
dismantle	dividend	dream	
dismiss	divine	dreary	eager
dismissal	divorce	dredge	eagle

earl	elect	emptiness	ensign
earlier	electricity	empty	entail
early	elegant	enable	entangle
earnest	elegy	enamored	enterprise
earring	element	enchant	entertain
earth	elementary	enclosure	enthusiasm
easement	elephant	encompass	entice
easily	eleven	encore	entire
Easter	elf	encourage	entomology
easy	elicit	encroach	entourage
eaves	eligible	encyclopedia	entrance
ebony	eliminate	endear	entreat
ebullient	elite	endeavor	entrée
eccentric	elixir	endorsement	entrepreneur
ecclesiastical	ellipse	endowment	entry
echo	elm	endurance	enunciate
eclipse	eloquent	enemy	envelop
economic	elucidate	energetic	envelope
economical	elude	enervate	enviable
ecstasy	elves	enforce	envies
ecumenical	else	enforceable	envious
eczema	emanate	engagement	environment
edge	embalm	engine	envy
edible	embarrassed	engineer	enwrap
edition	embassador	England	epic
editor	embellish	English	epicure
educable	embezzle	engrave	epidemic
educate	emblem	enhance	episode
eel	emboss	enjoyment	epitaph
effect	embrace	enlighten	epoch
effervescent	embroider	enliven	equally
efficacious	embryo	en masse	equilibrium
efficiency	emerald	enmesh	equinox
effort	emergency	enmity	equipped
egg	emigrant	ennoble	equity
ego	eminence	enormous	equivalent
eighteen	emissary	enough	erase
eighth	emollient	enquire	erection
Eisenhower	emotion	enrage	Erie
either	emperor	enrapture	ermine
eject	emphasis	enrich	errand
elaborate	empire	en route	erratic
elbow	employee	ensemble	erroneous

165

error	excursion	facetious	fathom
erudite	execute	facial	fatigue
escalator	executive	facilitate	fatten
escort	exercise	facing	fatuous
Eskimo	exert	facsimile	faucet
espionage	exhale	fact	fault
essay	exhaust	faction	favorable
essential	exhibit	factor	fawn
establish	exhilarate	factory	fear
estimate	exile	faculty	feasible
etch	exist	Fahrenheit	feast
eternity	existence	fail	feather
ethical	exodus	factual	feature
etiquette	exonerate	faille	February
Eucharist	exorbitant	faint	federal
eugenics	exotic	fairly	feebly
eulogy	expel	fairy	feel
eunuch	expendable	faith	feign
euphemism	expense	falcon	felicitate
European	experience	fall	fell
evening	expiration	fallacy	fellow
every	explanation	fallible	felony
everywhere	expletive	false	felt
evidence	explicit	falsetto	feminine
evil	exposal	falsify	fence
evolution	express	fame	ferment
exact	extempora-	familiar	ferocious
exactly	neous	family	ferry
exaggerate	extension	famine	fertile
exalt	extinct	famous	festival
examination	extracur-	fanatic	fetch
example	ricular	fanciful	**fetter**
exasperate	extraordinary	fancy	feud
exceed	extravagant	fantasy	feudal
excel	extreme	far	fever
excellent	extricate	farce	few
except	extrovert	farm	fiancé
excessive		farther	fiasco
excise	fable	fascinate	fibrous
excitable	fabric	fashion	fickle
excitement	fabulous	fasten	fiddle
exclude	façade	fatal	fidelity
excruciate	face	fateful	fidget

field	flexible	forecast	freak
fiend	flicker	forecastle	freckle
fierce	flies	foreclose	freight
fiery	flight	foregone	frequency
fight	flimsy	forehead	freshen
figure	flippant	foreign	Freud
file	flirt	foreman	friar
filet	flirtatious	foremost	fricassee
Filipino	float	foresee	friction
film	flock	foresight	Friday
filter	flood	forest	friend
final	floor	forever	fright
finance	Florida	forfeit	fringe
financial	florist	forge	frivolous
finely	flotilla	forgery	frock
finesse	flounce	forget	frontal
finger	flounder	forgive	frontiersman
fire	flourish	fork	frontispiece
firing	flower	formal	frown
firm	flown	formally	frozen
first	fluent	former	frugal
fission	fluid	formidable	fruitful
fitting	fluorescent	formula	fuchsia
fix	fluoride	forsake	fudge
flabbergast	fluoroscope	forsythia	fugitive
flaccid	flute	fortitude	fugue
flagging	fly	fortune	fulfill
flagrant	foam	forty	fumble
flake	focal	forum	fume
flame	focus	forward	function
flammable	foe	fossil	fundamental
flapper	foggy	fought	funeral
flatten	fold	found	fungus
flatter	foliage	fountain	funnel
flattery	folk	fourteen	funny
flatulent	follow	fourth	furious
flavor	folly	fox	furlough
flaw	foment	fragrance	furnish
flea	fondle	frail	furniture
fledgling	font	frame	furry
fleece	football	fraternal	further
fleet	forbid	fraudulent	fuselage
flesh	forcible	fraught	futile

future

gabardine
gadget
galaxy
gale
gallant
gallery
Gallic
gallon
gallop
gallows
gamble
game
gamma
  globulin
gamut
gangrene
garage
garbage
garden
gardener
garlic
garret
garrulous
gas
gaseous
gasket
gasoline
gauche
gaudy
gauge
gauze
gazelle
gazette
gear
geisha
gelatine
gendarme
genealogy
generally
generous
genetic

genial
genius
gentile
gentleman
gently
genuine
Georgia
geriatrics
German
germane
gesture
get
geyser
ghastly
ghetto
ghost
giant
giddy
gigantic
giggle
gigolo
gimmick
ginger
gingham
girdle
girl
giraffe
giveaway
glacial
glamorous
glance
glare
glass
glazier
gleam
glider
glimmer
glimpse
glitter
global
gloom
glorify
glossary

glutton
glycerin
gnarl
gnash
gnat
gnaw
gnome
goad
goal
goat
gobble
goblet
goddess
gondola
gone
good
goose
gopher
gorgeous
gospel
gossamer
gossip
gotten
gourd
gourmet
government
governor
gown
graceful
gracious
grade
gradual
grain
grammar
grand
grand-
    daughter
grandeur
graph
grass
grateful
gratitude
gravel

gravity
grease
greedy
green
greet
grenade
greyhound
grief
grievance
grieve
grille
grimace
groan
grocery
grope
gross
grotesque
group
grovel
grudge
gruesome
guarantee
guard
guess
guest
guidance
guide
guileless
guinea
guise
guitar
gullible
gunner
gurgle
gutter
guttural
guy
gymnasium
gynecology
gyp
gypsum
gypsy
gyroscope

168

haberdasher	hate	herbaceous	home
habilitate	haughty	heredity	homely
habituate	haunt	hereon	homemaker
hacienda	haven	heresy	homestead
hack	Hawaii	heretofore	homicide
haddock	hay	heritage	homogeneous
haggard	hazard	heroes	homogeneous
haggle	hazel	hermitage	honest
halcyon	head	herring	honey
half	headache	hers	honeydew
hallelujah	headdress	hesitate	honor
hallow	health	heteroge-	honorable
Halloween	heap	neous	honorary
hallucinate	hearse	hexagon	hood
halo	hearth	hiatus	hoof
halves	heartily	hibernate	hook
hamburger	hearty	hickory	hoping
hamlet	heat	hidden	horizon
hammer	heathen	hideous	hormone
handful	heave	hierarchy	hornet
handicap	heaven	hieroglyphic	horoscope
handkerchief	heavy	highbrow	horrendous
handle	heckle	highness	horrible
happen	hectic	hilarious	horrified
happily	hedge	hindrance	horror
harangue	hedonist	hindsight	hors
harass	head	hinge	d'oeuvres
harbor	heifer	hippo-	horse
hardboiled	height	potamus	horsy
hardening	heinous	hireling	horticulture
harebrained	heiress	history	hose
harem	heirloom	hitch	hosiery
harlequin	helicopter	hoax	hospital
harmonious	hell	hobby	hostage
harness	hello	hockey	hostile
harridan	helmet	hodgepodge	hotel
harried	hemisphere	hoist	hound
harsh	hemoglobin	holiday	household
harvest	hemorrhage	holiness	houses
hassle	henceforth	hollandaise	housewife
hasten	henna	hollow	housing
hatch	herald	holocaust	hovel
hatchet	herb	homage	hover
			howl

huckleberry	Iceland	immature	impromptu
huddle	ichthyology	immeasur-	improvement
huge	icing	able	impugn
humane	icon	immediate	inaccurate
humble	iconoclast	immemorable	inane
humiliate	idea	immense	inappropriate
humility	ideal	immigrant	inapt
humming	identical	imminent	inaugurate
humor	identify	immobile	inauspicious
humorous	ideology	immoral	incalculable
hundred	ides	immortal	incandescent
hunger	idiom	immune	incarnate
hungry	idiosyncrasy	impair	incendiary
hunting	idiot	impartial	incentive
hurdle	idolater	impasse	incessant
hurl	idyllic	impassioned	incest
hurray	ignominious	impatient	incident
hurricane	ignorant	impeach	incidentally
husband	ignore	impeccable	incriminator
hussy	iguana	impecunious	incipient
hustle	Iliad	impede	inclement
hybrid	illegal	impel	inclination
hydrangea	illegible	impenetrable	include
hydrant	illegitimate	imperial	incognito
hydraulic	illicit	impersonal	inconsolable
hydrogen	Illinois	imperturb-	incorporate
hydrophobia	illiterate	able	incorrigible
hyena	illness	impetus	increase
hygiene	illogical	impiety	incredible
hymnal	illuminate	impinge	increment
hypertension	illusion	impious	incumbent
hyphen	illustrate	implacable	incurred
hypnotist	image	implement	incurring
hypocrisy	imaginable	implicit	indebted
hypocrite	imagination	imply	indecent
hypodermic	imagine	impolite	indecorous
hypothetical	imbalance	importance	indefensible
hysteria	imbecile	impossi-	indelible
	imbibe	bility	independent
	imbue	impotent	index
ibex	imitation	impresario	Indian
ice	immaculate	impress	indicative
iceberg	immaterial	impression	indictment

indifferent	ingenious	insulate	irascible
indigenous	ingratiate	intangible	iridescence
indigestible	ingredient	integral	iron
indigo	inhabitant	integrate	irrational
indiscrim-	inhale	intellectual	irreconcilable
inate	inherit	intelligence	irredeemable
indistinguish-	inhibition	intemperate	irregular
able	initial	intensify	irrelevance
individually	initiative	intention	irrelevant
indoctrinate	injection	intercede	irresistible
indolent	injury	intercept	irresponsible
indomitable	injustice	intercession	irrevocable
inducement	innate	intercourse	irrigate
inebriate	inner	interest	irritable
ineffable	innervate	interesting	Islam
inefficacious	innocence	interfere	island
inefficient	innocuous	interference	isle
inert	innovate	interlude	isolate
inertia	innuendo	intermediate	isotope
inescapable	inoculate	intermittent	Israel
inevitable	inordinate	internal	issuance
inexorable	inquire	interpolate	issue
infallible	insanity	interpret	isthmus
infamous	inscrutable	interrogate	Italian
infancy	insect	interrupt	itch
infant	inseparable	interview	item
infection	inside	intimate	ivory
inference	insight	intoxicate	ivy
inferior	insipid	intricacy	
infidelity	insistent	intrigue	
infiltrate	insolent	introduce	
infinitely	insoluble	invalid	jackal
infinitive	inspiration	invasion	jackass
infirmary	instance	inveigle	jacket
inflammable	instantaneous	investigate	jackknife
inflation	instead	inveterate	jade
inflection	instigate	invigorate	jagged
influence	instinct	invisible	jaguar
information	institute	invite	jail
infrared	instrument	invoice	jalopy
infrequent	insubordi-	invoke	janitor
infuriate	nate	inward	January
infuse	insufferable	iodine	Japanese

171

jardiniere	jungle	klieg	language
jargon	junior	knack	languish
jasmine	jurisdiction	knapsack	languor
jaundice	jury	knee	lanolin
jazz	just	knickknack	lantern
jealous	justice	knife	lapel
jeep	justify	knives	larceny
Jeffersonian	juvenile	knob	large
jelly		knock	larkspur
jeopardy		knoll	larynx
jerk	kaleidoscope	knotted	lascivious
jersey	kangaroo	knout	lassie
Jesuit	kaput	knowledge	lassitude
jettison	katydid	knuckle	lasso
jetty	kayak	kosher	làtch
jewelry	keel	Kremlin	late
jewels	keen		lately
jibe	Kennedy		latent
jigger	kennel	label	latitude
jimmy	kept	labor	latticework
jitterbug	kerchief	laboratory	laudable
jobber	kernel	labyrinth	laughable
jockey	kerosene	lace	laughter
jocular	kettle	lacerate	launch
jodhpurs	key	lachrymose	laundry
Johnson	khaki	lacing	laurel
joker	Khrushchev	lackey	lavaliere
jolly	kibitzer	laconic	lavatory
jostle	kick	lacquer	lavender
jotting	kidney	ladder	lawn
journal	killer	ladies	lawyer
journey	kilowatt	ladle	laxative
jovial	kimono	laggard	laziness
joyous	kindergarten	lagging	leader
jubilant	kindness	laid	leaf
jubilee	kindle	lake	league
judge	kindred	lambaste	leakage
judgment	kingdom	lame	leaped
judicial	kipper	lamentable	learn
judiciary	kissed	laminate	lease
juggler	kitchen	lance	leather
juice	kitten	landlord	leave
juncture	kleptomania	landscape	leaven

leaves	libido	lively	ludicrous
lecture	library	livery	luggage
ledger	libretto	lives	lukewarm
legal	license	lizard	lullaby
legalize	licentious	loafer	luminescent
legend	licorice	loathe	lunacy
legerdemain	liege	lobby	lunatic
legging	lieu	localize	luncheonette
legible	lieutenant	locket	lure
legion	lifeboat	locomotive	luscious
legislature	lifetime	locust	lustrous
legitimate	ligament	lodge	lute
leisure	light	logarithm	luxuriant
leisurely	likable	logic	luxury
lemonade	likely	loneliness	lying
length	likeness	lonely	lymph
lenient	lilac	lonesome	Lyndon
lens	lily	longevity	lynx
lent	limb	longitude	lyric
leopard	limber	loquacious	
leprechaun	lime	lord	
leprosy	limelight	lore	macadam
lesbian	limit	Lorelei	macaroni
lessen	Lincoln	lorgnette	macaroon
lethal	linear	lose	machete
lethargy	linen	loss	Machiavel-
let's	lingerie	lotion	lian
letter	linguist	lottery	machinery
lettered	linkage	loud	mackerel
lettuce	limousine	lounge	mackintosh
letup	linoleum	lousy	madame
level	lion	lout	mademoiselle
leveler	liquefy	louver	madras
levitation	liquid	Louvre	magazine
lewd	liquor	lovable	maggot
lexicon	lissome	love	magic
liability	listen	lovely	magistrate
liaison	litany	loving	magnet
liar	literacy	lowbrow	magnificence
libel	literature	loyal	magnitude
liberal	little	lubricate	maharajah
liberalism	liturgical	lucid	mahogany
libidinous	livelihood	luck	maidenly

173

maintenance
major
majority
malady
malediction
malfeasance
malice
malicious
malign
malinger
malleable
making
mambo
mammal
mammoth
manacle
manageable
manager
mandatory
maneuver
mange
manger
mania
manicure
manifesto
manifold
manner
mansion
mantelpiece
manufacture
manuscript
many
maple
maraschino
maraud
marble
margarine
margin
marijuana
marine
maritime
market
marmalade

maroon
marquis
marquise
marriage
marriageable
married
marrow
marry
martini
martyr
marvelous
masculine
masonry
masquerade
Massachu-
   setts
massacre
massage
masseur
massive
master
masticate
material
maternity
mathematics
matinée
maître d'
matriarch
matrimony
matronly
matter
mattress
maturation
mature
maudlin
mausoleum
maverick
maximum
maybe
mayonnaise
meadow
meager
meanness

meant
measles
measure
mechanic
mechanize
medal
medallion
meddle
Medicare
medicine
medieval
mediocre
Mediter-
   ranean
medium
medley
megalomania
melancholy
mélange
melon
mellow
melodious
melodrama
membrane
memento
memoir
memorable
memorial
memory
menace
menagerie
menial
menstruate
mental
mention
menu
mercenary
merchandise
mercy
merely
merger
meringue
merit

merrily
messenger
mesmerize
messy
metal
metallic
metamor-
   phosis
metaphor
meteor
Methodist
metropolitan
mezzanine
miasma
mice
microscope
midday
middle
mien
migrate
mileage
military
militia
millennium
millinery
millionaire
mince
mineral
mingle
miniature
minimum
minister
Minnesota
minority
minus
minuscule
minute
minutia
miracle
mirage
mirror
miscella-
   neous

mischief	monotonous	mutiny	negative
mischievous	monsieur	myopia	neglect
misconduct	monstrous	myrtle	negligee
miser	month	mysterious	negligence
miserable	mope	mystery	negotiate
misery	morality	mysticism	Negroes
misfortune	morgue	mystify	Nehru
mishap	Mormon	mythical	neighbor
mislaid	morocco		neither
misogyny	morphine		nephew
missile	morsel	nagged	nepotism
mission	mortgage	nail	nervous
Mississippi	mortally	naïve	nestle
misspell	mortify	naïveté	neuralgia
misstate	mortuary	naked	neuritis
mistake	mosaic	nameless	neurologist
mistress	mosque	naphtha	neurotic
mitten	mosquito	narcissistic	neutral
mixture	mossy	narcotics	neutralize
mnemonic	motif	narration	new
moan	motion	narrative	next
moat	motor	narrow	Niagara
mobilize	mottled	nascent	nibble
moccasin	mournful	nastiness	nicely
mockery	movement	nasturtium	niche
model	mucilage	national	nickel
modern	mucous	naturally	nicotine
modest	mucus	nature	niece
modifier	muddy	nausea	night
modulate	Muham-	navigable	nihilism
moire	madan	navy	nil
moisture	Mulatto	Nazi	nimble
molecule	mulish	near	nineteen
molestation	multiply	neat	ninety
mollify	mundane	nebulous	ninth
momentous	murderer	necessary	nipple
monarch	murmur	necessity	Nixon
monastery	muscle	neck	nobleman
money	museum	neckerchief	noblesse
monkey	music	necromancy	oblige
monogamist	muslin	nectarine	nocturnal
monopoly	mustache	needle	noise
monotone	mustard	nefarious	noisome

nominate	obbligato	often	orchid
nonchalant	obedience	ogle	ordinary
nonentity	obese	ogre	ordinance
normal	obey	oil	organ
north	obituary	ointment	organization
northerly	object	old	orgasm
nosegay	objectionable	olfactory	orgy
nostalgic	oblige	olive	origin
notable	oblique	Olympic	original
notary	obnoxious	omelet	ornament
notch	obscene	ominous	orphan
nothing	obsequious	omissible	orthodox
notice	observance	omission	oscillate
noticeable	obsession	omit	osculatory
notion	obsolescent	omniscient	ossify
notorious	obsolete	omnivorous	ostensible
nourish	obstacle	once	ostentatious
nouveau	obstetrician	onerous	ostrich
riche	obstinate	opaque	ought
novel	obvious	open	ounce
novice	occasion	openness	ours
nowhere	occasional	opera	ourselves
noxious	occupancy	operate	oust
nuclear	occupant	operator	outer
nucleus	occupied	operetta	outrageous
nudity	occur	ophthal-	outsider
nuisance	occurrence	mology	outward
nullification	ocean	opinion	ovary
numb	oceanography	opium	overrate
numerous	octopus	opponent	overreach
numskull	oculist	opportune	overrun
nunnery	odd	opportunity	overseer
nuptial	odor	oppose	overt
nurse	odorous	oppressor	overture
nursemaid	Odyssey	optician	overwhelm
nurseries	Oedipus	optional	overwrought
nutrition	off	optimism	oxygen
nutty	offense	opus	oyster
nymph	offer	oracle	
	offering	orange	
	office	orator	Pacific
oar	official	orbit	pacifist
oath	officious	orchestra	pacify

package
pact
padre
paean
pageant
pagoda
paid
paisley
pajama
Pakistan
palace
palatable
palate
palatial
palisade
pallbearer
pall-mall
palm
palmistry
palpable
palpitate
palsy
pamphlet
panacea
panatella
pancake
pandemo-
   nium
panel
panicky
panorama
pansy
pantomime
papacy
papier-
   mâché
paprika
parable
parabola
parachute
parade
paradise
paradox

paraffin
paragraph
parakeet
parallel
paralysis
paralyze
paramecium
paramount
paranoia
parapher-
   nalia
paraphrase
paraplegic
parasite
paratrooper
parcel
parcheesi
parenthesis
parfait
pari-mutuel
parish
parity
parliament
parlor
Parmesan
parochial
parody
parole
parquet
parrot
parson
partial
participate
participle
particle
particular
parties
partisan
partition
partitive
partner
passable
passage

passé
passion
passive
passport
pastel
pasteurize
pastime
pasting
pastor
pastrami
pastry
pâté de
   foie gras
patent
paternal
patient
patio
patriot
patriotism
patrol
patron
pathos
pattern
pavement
pavilion
paving
peach
peanut
peasant
pecan
peccadillo
peculiar
pecuniary
pedestal
pedestrian
pediatrics
pedigree
peevish
peignoir
pellet
penal
penalty
pencil

pendulum
penetrate
penicillin
peninsula
penitent
penitentiary
penknife
penmanship
pennant
penniless
Pennsylvania
Pentagon
Pentecostal
penurious
people
per annum
perceive
percent
percolator
percussion
perennial
perfect
perforate
perform
perfunctory
perhaps
peril
perimeter
period
periphery
periscope
perish
perjury
permanent
permeate
permissible
permit
peroxide
perpen-
   dicular
perpetrate
perpetual
persecute

177

persevere	phonics	pinup	plentiful
persistence	phonograph	pioneer	plethora
person	phony	pious	pleurisy
personal	phosphate	piping	pliable
perspica-	phospho-	pistachio	pliers
cious	rescence	piston	plight
perspiration	phosphorus	pitfall	plumber
perspire	photograph	pittance	plural
persuade	phrase	pitiful	plus
pertinent	physically	Pittsburgh	plutonium
perturb	physician	pituitary	pneumatic
pervade	physics	pivot	pneumonia
perverse	physiognomy	pizza	pocket
pervert	physiology	placard	pocketbook
peso	physio-	placate	poem
pessimist	therapy	placebo	poet
pesticide	physique	placement	pogrom
petal	pianist	placid	poignant
petite	piano	plagiarism	poinsettia
petition	piazza	plague	poise
petrify	pica	plaid	poison
petroleum	picayune	planet	polar
petticoat	piccolo	planetarium	Polaris
petulant	picket	plasma	polarize
pew	pickle	plastic	Polaroid
phantom	picnic	plateau	polemic
pharaoh	piece	platform	police
pharmacy	pierce	platinum	policy
phase	piety	platitude	polio
pheno-	pigment	platonic	polish
barbital	pilfer	platoon	polite
phenomenon	piigrim	platter	politics
Philadelphia	piling	plausible	polka
philanderer	pillage	plaza	pollen
philanthropy	pillar	plea	pollute
philately	pillbox	plead	polyethylene
philharmonic	pilory	pleasant	polygamy
Philippines	pilot	please	polygon
philosophy	pimento	pleasure	pomade
phlegm	pimple	pleat	pompadour
phobia	pincers	plebiscite	pompous
Phoenix	pineapple	pledge	Pontiff
phonetic	pinnacle	plenary	popular

porcelain	predecessor	prevalent	progeny
pornography	predicament	prevaricate	prognosis
portable	predicate	prevention	program
portfolio	predict	preview	progress
portrait	predictable	previous	prohibit
position	predominant	priceless	project
positive	preeminent	prickly	prolific
posse	prefabricate	priest	prologue
possess	preface	primary	promenade
possession	prefer	primeval	promiscuous
possible	preference	primitive	promise
postage	pregnant	princess	promissory
postal	prejudice	priority	prompt
postpone	preliminary	prism	pronuncia-
posture	prelude	prison	tion
potato	premature	privacy	propaganda
potassium	premier	private	propagate
potential	premise	privilege	propel
potpourri	premium	probable	proper
pottery	premonition	problem	property
poultry	preoccupa-	procedure	prophecy
pounce	tion	proceed	prophet
pour	preparation	process	proponent
pout	prepare	procession	proportion
poverty	preponderant	proclaim	proposal
powder	preposition	procrastinate	propose
practical	preposterous	procreate	proposition
practice	prerogative	proctor	proprietor
prairie	Presbyterian	procure	propriety
prayer	prescribe	prodigious	propulsion
preamble	prescription	prodigy	prosaic
precarious	present	produce	prosecute
precaution	preserve	product	prospect
precede	preside	profess	prospective
precedent	president	profession	prospectus
precept	pressure	professor	prostate
precinct	prestige	proffer	prostitute
precious	presume	proficient	protagonist
precipitate	presumption	profile	protect
précis	pretend	profit	protégé
precise	prettify	profligate	protein
preclude	pretty	profuse	protest
precocious	prevail	progenitor	Protestant

179

protocol	puppet	radical	ravel
proton	purchase	radioed	raven
protoplasm	pure	radish	raw
prototype	purge	radium	rayon
protrude	purple	radius	raze
proud	purpose	raffia	razor
prove	purse	raffle	reach
provide	pursue	raft	reaction
providence	pursuit	raged	reactor
provoke	pusillani-	ragged	reader
proximity	mous	raglan	readily
proxy	putrefy	ragout	ready
prude	putrid	raid	realism
pry	putt	railing	reality
psalm	puzzle	raiment	realize
pseudo	pyramid	rain	really
pseudonym	Pyrex	rainy	realm
psyche	pyromaniac	raisin	reap
psychiatrist	pyrotechnics	rakish	reason
psychic	Pyrrhic	rally	reasonable
psychoanaly-	victory	ramble	rebait
sis		ramification	rebate
psychology		rampage	rebel
psychosis	qualify	rampant	rebellion
ptomaine	quality	rancid	rebuke
public	quantity	random	rebuttal
pudding	quarantine	range	recalcitrate
pudgy	quarrel	rankle	recapitulate
pueblo	questionnaire	ransom	recede
puerile	quick	rapacious	receipt
Puerto Rico	quiver	rarely	receivable
pulchritude	quizzical	rarity	receive
pullet	rabble	raspberry	recent
pulmonary	rabies	ratable	reception
pulpit	raccoon	ratchet	recess
pulverize	racial	rather	recession
pumpernickel	racism	ratio	recipe
pumpkin	racket	ration	reciprocal
punctual	racketeer	rationalize	reciprocity
punctuate	raconteur	rattle	recital
puncture	racy	rattlesnake	recitation
pungent	radial	raucous	reckless
punitive	radiant	ravage	reckon

reclamation	regiment	remonstrate	reputable
recluse	region	remorseful	require
recognize	register	remote	requisite
recommend	regression	removable	requittal
recompense	regrettable	removal	resalable
reconnais-	regular	remunerate	rescind
sance	regulate	renaissance	research
reconnoiter	regurgitate	renascence	resemblance
record	rehabilitate	rendezvous	resent
recoup	rehearsal	renegade	reservation
recovery	rehearse	renege	reservoir
recreation	Reich	renew	residence
recriminatory	reindeer	reparable	residual
recruit	reject	repartee	residue
rectal	rejoice	repeal	resign
rectangle	rejuvenate	renovate	resilience
rectify	relation	reorganize	resin
recuperate	relative	repair	resistance
recurrence	relax	repeat	resistible
redemption	release	repel	resolution
redden	relegate	repellent	resolve
reduce	relentless	repercussion	resonance
reducible	relevant	repertory	resort
redundant	reliable	repetition	resource
reenforce	reliant	repetitive	respectable
reentry	relied	replacement	respirator
refer	relief	replete	respite
reference	relieve	replica	responsible
refinement	religious	reply	restaurant
reflection	relinquish	repository	restoration
reflex	relish	reprehensible	result
reform	reluctance	represent	resume
reformation	rely	repressed	resumption
refrain	remain	reprieve	resurrection
refrigerator	remedial	reprimand	resuscitate
refugee	remedy	reprisal	retail
refurbish	remember	reprise	retain
refusal	reminisce	reprobate	retaliate
regal	remission	reproduce	reticent
regale	remit	reptile	retina
regardless	remittance	republic	retire
regency	remittent	republican	retirement
regime	remnant	repugn	retouch

retribution	rifle	rough	sarsaparilla
retrieve	right	roulette	satellite
retrogression	righteous	routine	satisfaction
retrospect	rigid	roving	satisfactory
retroussé	rigmarole	royal	Saturday
reveal	rigor	royally	sauerkraut
reveille	rigorous	rubber	sausage
revelation	ringer	rudder	saving
revenge	rinsing	rude	scarce
revenue	riot	ruler	scarcely
reverent	riotous	rumble	scarcity
reverie	ripe	rummage	scare
reversible	ripen	rummy	scene
revert	ripple	rumor	scenic
revise	rise	runner	schedule
revision	rising	running	scheme
revival	risqué	rupture	schism
revocation	ritual	rural	scholar
revolt	rival	russet	scholastic
revolution	rivet	Russia	schooner
rewrite	roam	rustic	science
rhapsody	roaring	rustle	scissors
rheostat	roast	rye	Scripture
rhetoric	robbery		scythe
rheumatism	robin	Sabbath	season
rhinestone	robot	sabotage	secede
rhinoceros	rock	saccharin	secession
Rhode	Rockefeller	sacrament	secretary
Island	rocket	sacred	sedan
rhododen-	rococo	sacrifice	seduce
dron	Roentgen	sacrilegious	seeing
rhubarb	rogue	safety	seem
rhumba	roguish	said	segregate
rhyme	romance	salad	seize
rhythm	roofs	salami	seizure
ribald	Roosevelt	salary	seldom
ribbon	rosary	Salk vaccine	select
rickety	rose	salmon	selfish
ricksha	rosin	salve	selves
riddance	rotary	sandwich	semester
riddle	rotten	sanitation	senator
ridge	roué	sapphire	senior
ridiculous	rouge	sarcastic	sensitive

separate	sofa	submarine	symmetry
September	soften	subordinate	sympathy
sergeant	solar	subpoena	symphony
series	solder	subscription	symptom
sermon	soldier	subsistence	syndicate
service	solemn	subtle	synthetic
serviceable	sophisticate	suburb	syringe
settee	sophomore	suburban	syrup
seventh	sorrow	succeed	system
several	sorry	success	
sexy	southern	successor	
sheath	souvenir	succinct	tablet
sheik	sovereign	suede	taboo
shelves	Soviet	sufficient	tabulate
shepherd	Union	suffix	tacit
sherbet	spaghetti	suffrage	tackle
sheriff	Spaniard	suggest	tact
shield	special	suggestion	tactics
shillelagh	specialty	summary	taffeta
shining	specify	superfluous	tailor
shipment	specimen	superintendent	taint
shipped	speech	supersede	Taiwan
should	spirit	supplies	taking
shoulders	sponsor	supply	talent
shouldn't	stalk	suppose	tangent
shove	starboard	suppress	tangible
shriek	statement	surface	tantalize
siege	stating	surgeon	tantrum
sieve	statistic	surgery	target
signature	status	surmise	tariff
significant	stealthy	surplus	tarnish
silence	stomach	surprise	tasting
silhouette	stopped	surround	tattered
similar	strait jacket	surveillance	tattle
sincere	strength	survey	tattoo
sincerely	strenuous	survival	tawdry
situation	strenuously	survive	teach
sixth	stretch	suspicion	tearful
skeleton	strictly	sword	technical
skeptical	struggle	syllable	technique
slaughter	study	syllabus	tedious
socialist	studying	symbol	teenager
society	suave	symmetrical	telegram

telephone	testament	tight	torrent
television	testify	till	torrid
temerity	testimony	timid	torque
temperament	tetanus	timorous	totaling
temperance	textbook	timpani	tour
temperature	textile	tin	tragedy
template	texture	tingle	transfer
temporarily	Thailand	tinsel	treachery
temporary	theater	tiny	tremendous
tempt	theft	tip-off	treasurer
temptation	their	tirade	tried
tenable	theirs	tithe	tries
tenacious	theme	titillate	triplicate
tenacity	themselves	title	triumph
tenant	theology	titular	trouble
tendency	theorem	toady	truly
tendentious	theory	tobacco	Truman
tendon	therapeutic	toboggan	truthfully
tenement	thermo-	today	tryst
tenet	nuclear	toga	Tuesday
Tennessee	thermostat	together	tulip
tenor	thesaurus	toilet	tumult
tension	these	token	turpentine
tentacle	thesis	tolerant	turpitude
tentative	thief	toll	twelfth
tenuous	thieves	tomato	tying
tepee	thirsty	tomb	type
tepid	thirteen	tombstone	typewriter
tequila	thorough	tomorrow	tyrant
terminal	though	tongue	
terminate	thousand	tonic	
termite	thread	tonight	ubiquitous
terms	threat	tonnage	ukulele
terrain	threshold	tonsil	ulcer
terrestrial	thrifty	tonsillectomy	ulterior
terrible	thrilling	tooth	ultimate
terribly	thriving	topic	ultimatum
terrific	throat	Torah	umbilical
terrify	thug	toreador	umbrage
territorial	thwart	torment	umbrella
territory	tiara	tornado	umpire
terror	tickle	torpedo	**unacceptable**
terse	tier	torpor	unanimous

184

unavoidable	unify	valid	verily
uncertain	unilateral	valor	verity
uncle	unimpeach-	valuable	vermin
uncommon	able	valve	vermouth
unconditional	unique	vandal	vernacular
unconscious	unison	vanilla	versatile
uncontrol-	unit	vanish	verse
lable	Unitarian	vanity	versification
uncouth	United	vapid	versify
unctuous	Nations	vaquero	versus
undeniable	United	variable	vertebra
underground	States	variety	vertebral
underprivi-	unity	various	vertebrate
leged	universe	vase	vertical
understand	universally	vassal	vessel
undertaker	university	Vatican	vested
underwrite	unkempt	vaudeville	vestibule
underwriter	unknowable	vector	vestige
undesirable	unmistakable	vegetable	veterans
undoubtedly	unnamed	vehement	veterinary
undress	unnatural	vehicle	vetoes
undue	unnecessary	veil	vex
unduly	unoccupied	vein	viable
undying	unorganized	velocity	vibrant
unearned	unpleasant	venal	vice
unearth	unpopular	veneer	vicinity
uneasy	unprece-	venerable	vicious
unemployed	dented	veneration	victim
unequal	unprejudiced	Venetian	victory
unequivocal	unprincipled	vengeance	victuals
unerring	until	Venice	Viet Nam
unfair	usable	venom	vigil
unfavorable	used to	venomous	vigilance
unfinished	useful	ventilate	vigor
unfit	using	ventilation	vigorous
unforgettable	usually	ventrilo-	vilify
unfortunate	U Thant	quist	village
unfriendly		veracity	villain
ungodly		verbal	vindicate
ungrateful	vaccination	verbally	vinegar
unhealthy	vacillate	verifiable	violet
unholy	vacuum	verification	violin
uniform	valentine	verify	viper

virgin
virtue
virulence
virulent
visage
visible
vital
vitally
vitamin
vitiate
vivid
vocabulary
voice
volume
voluntary
vomit
vulgar

wafer
wagon
waken
wallet
walnut
wanton
warble
warden
warehouse
warning
warp
warranty
warrior
wary

wassail
wastage
waylaid
wealth
weapon
weather
wedding
Wednesday
weird
welcome
welfare
western
whereof
whether
while
whipper-
    snapper
whippoorwill
whisk broom
whiskey
whisper
whistle
white
who
wholesale
wholesome
wicked
wild
wilderness
wince
wintry
Wisconsin
wisdom

wither
withhold
wives
wizard
wolves
womb
women
won
wondrous
world
worm
worship
worsted
wound
wrangle
wrath
wreath
wreck
wrestle
wretch
wriggle
wrinkle
wrist
writhe
writing
written
wrong

Xavier
Xmas
X-ray
xylophone

yacht
yearned
yellow
Yemen
yeoman
yesterday
yield
yodel
yoga
yogi
yogurt (or:
    yoghurt)
yonder
you all
youngster
yours
yourself

zeal
zenith
zephyr
Zeus
zinc
zither
Zodiac
zoology